I Love Christmas

Christmas Messages

by

Evangelist John R. Rice
Editor, THE SWORD OF THE LORD

Sword of the Lord Publishers
Murfreesboro, Tennessee

Printed in U.S.A.

PREFACE

Best wishes for a happy Christmas. May yours be the joy of loved ones about you, of presents that represent loving thoughts. May you have the beautiful Christmas cards from those who are away, and the gifts under the Christmas tree. May the Christmas table be loaded with good things to eat. Yes, we wish you a happy Christmas.

But far more important than these pleasant trappings and customs of Christmas is that you have the Christ of Christmas and His joy. So we wish that the green of the Christmas tree may picture eternal life springing up in your heart. May the lights strung there by loving hands picture Christ, the Light of the world, shining in your heart.

May the joyful message of the angels given at the first Christmas ring in your heart, "...a Saviour, which is Christ the Lord!" Shepherds, wise men, the holy family—you may be as happy as any of them, and I pray that you may be, at this glad season.

The Christmas joy does not depend on the outward trappings of Christmas. You may be lonely, poor, and cold, neglected by the children, forgotten by your friends, yet may have the glad Christmas joy in your heart as Paul had, shut up in prison cells at Rome! Be sure to open your heart and let the dear Lord Jesus make it a happy Christmastime for you. These messages are about Him and the purpose of the book will be fulfilled if readers open their hearts and homes to the dear Lord Jesus, born in a stable, laid in a manger, who then grew up to die on the cross for our sins and rose from the dead to be our ever-living Saviour.

In His dear name, happy Christmas!

JOHN R. RICE

CONTENTS

1 Love Christmas

"One man esteemeth one day above another: another esteemeth every day alike. Let every man be fully persuaded in his own mind. He that regardeth the day, regardeth it unto the Lord; and he that regardeth not the day, to the Lord he doth not regard it..."—Rom. 14:5,6a.

I LOVE the Christmas season. I find great joy in preaching on the Christmas themes of the angels, the shepherds, the manger, the virgin birth, the wise men. I have great joy in the Christmas carols. There is a joyful, happy note of worship in our home, and thank God, in my heart, through the Christmastime. I love the gathering together of my loved ones and family for Christmas. I love to give gifts, and I rejoice to be remembered by my loved ones and friends. I love the Christmas season.

Perhaps my own feeling is colored somewhat by the fact that for many years, I have been away from home most of the year, but at the Christmas season, when churches and groups of churches do not want revivals, I have been at home with my family. That makes it extra precious to me.

It makes me sad that many people do not enjoy Christmas. Some devoted Christians feel sour, cantanker-

1

ous, and full of objections about Christmas. To them I would say the words of Scripture, that if you regard the day, regard it unto the Lord. And if you do not regard the day, Christmas, then be sure that you are Christian about it as unto the Lord. But let nobody be judging and criticizing others for honest, worshipful, spiritual, and loving attitudes about Christmas.

I want to answer some of the objections about Christmas.

1. They Say Christmas Is Not Christ's Birthday.

Actually, no one knows exactly when Christ was born. The Bible does not say. There are no other trustworthy sources from which we can learn when Christ was born. So, some people think it is therefore wrong to observe Christmas. But that does not necessarily follow. I knew a little girl born on February 29, leap year. Now would it be wrong for that little girl to observe a birthday on the last day of February on other years when February had only twenty-eight days? Or would it be a sin for her to observe her birthday, or for others to observe her birthday anytime except on leap year. No, the important fact was not the precise date, February 29, but that another year had gone by for which people should praise God, and the little girl had grown a year older, and that fact ought to be recognized by those who loved her.

Would you say that it is wrong to have Thanksgiving day on a certain Thursday in November, when not all of our blessings have come on that day? Or would you say it is wrong to set a more convenient day if all of us should agree that it was proper and convenient to have a national day of thanksgiving? Whatever the day, it is still right for people to agree on a time when we would publicly thank God and officially, as a nation, express our gratitude to the Father of Mercies for all of His goodness to us. The important thing is not what day of the calendar, but whether or not we honor God on the day.

December 25 is as close to the birthday of Christ as we can come. We love the dear Lord Jesus, we want everybody to remember His birth, we want to teach our children about the Baby in the manger, about the wise men who came from the East to worship Him, about the angel's announcement to Mary and the angel chorus who told the shepherds. And why is not December 25 as good a day for that as any other? Do you think it is wrong to remember the birth of Christ on the day which is as close as we can come to the birthday of Christ?

2. Christmas Means Only Christ's Mass, a Catholic Holiday to Many.

We are told that Christmas comes from Christ's Mass, that it was instituted by Catholics, and that therefore good Protestants ought not to observe it. That objection seems a little foolish to me. Nearly all of the names we have inherited from heathen people. Many of the names of cities, towns, counties, and rivers in America are Indian names. But when we see the Susquehanna River, or Shawnee, Oklahoma, or Coman-che, Texas, we are not thinking about the Indians, and the names have no connotation of heathendom. Names mean what they mean, no matter what the origin.

The Seventh-Day Adventists sometimes make much of the fact that the name of our day, Sunday, comes from the worship of the sun. I reply that Saturday is named for the god Saturn. But nobody has any reference to the sun when they use the word Sunday or when they worship on Sunday, and no one has any reference to the god Saturn when they work or serve on Saturday. It is foolish to make an artificial distinction when none exists in the mind and heart of people who observe Christmas. January was named for the Roman god Janus. Are Christians therefore sinning when they call the month by that name? To every sensible person, Christmas simply means Christmas. It does not convey any kind of mass. Catholics may observe it with mass, but Protestants do not.

3. It Is Claimed That Christmas Was a Former Heathen Holiday.

I shall not go into the argument pro and con, but it is not well proven, I think, that Christmas was a former heathen holiday. But if it were, that would not change the fact that heathen people did something on every day, and we cannot do away with all the days that heathen people used, whether for worship, or for ceremonies about sowing, or about reaping, or about the solstices, or the new moons. We use the same sun that heathen people worshiped, and we love the sun rising and sun setting, though we do not have the heathen ceremonies about that. This argument is not important.

I held a blessed revival campaign in the Binghamton Theater, Binghamton, New York, sponsored by eight churches, in 1936. The fact that here people had seen lewd movies, or burlesque shows, or legitimate theater productions, did not change the fact that now the building was used for the glory of God and souls were saved. I myself am under new management, too. Once the Devil lived within; now Jesus Christ lives within. So if heathen people used the twenty-fifth of December for idolatry, why should Christians not use it now to honor Jesus

Christ and His birth? If we have any day to represent Christ, it will be a day somebody else has used for bad purposes; but, thank God, all the days belong to Christ now, and none of them belong to heathen gods. Why should any Christian be grieved if I especially think about the birth of Christ on December 25? Is that a worse sin than working to make money on that day? Why should anybody grieve if I sing Christmas carols, if I have a happy celebration with a feast, and if I go over the Bible story of the birth of Christ and teach it to my children, on Christmas day? Does that dishonor God? Do you think you would honor God more by having less Scripture, less songs, less of the spirit of giving, less manifestation of love for others? I do not think so! All the days belong to Jesus Christ, and December 25 should be used to honor Him, too, in one way or another.

4. Christmas Trees and Decorations Are Counted by Some an Abomination.

Some have even said that the Bible forbids the use of Christmas trees. A woman called my attention to Jeremiah 10:3,4, thinking it referred to Christmas trees. That Scripure says:

> *"For the customs of the people are vain: for one cut-teth a tree out of the forest, the work of the hands of the workman, with the axe. They deck it with silver and with gold; they fasten it with nails and with hammers, that it move not."*

But does that Scripture talk about the Christmas tree? Not at all. It speaks of an idol made out of wood, covered ith silver and gold. The next verse says:

> *"They are upright as the palm tree, but speak not: they must needs be borne, because they cannot go. Be not*

5

afraid of them; for they cannot do evil, neither also is it in them do good."

The idol is not a real god; it cannot see, nor hear, nor do good, nor bad. So verse 8 below says that "the stock [or idol] is a doctrine of vanities." And the rest of the Scripture tells how elaborately and expensively the idol is made out of silver and gold, and dressed in purple. And then verse 10 tells us: But the Lord is the true God, he is the living God..." Verse 11 says: The gods that have not made the heavens and the earth, even they shall perish from the earth...."

No, the Bible does not forbid Christmas trees.

It is true that heathen people have sometimes worshiped trees. They have also worshiped animals, worshiped the wind, worshiped the ocean, worshiped the sun. But there is no worship of idols in setting up a green Christmas tree as a decoration, as a symbol of joy and gladness.

Is there harm in decorating the house with holly, or mistletoe, or other evergreen? No more than decorating the house with pumpkins, and oak leaves, and cornstalks at Thanksgiving time! No more than decorating graves with flowers on Memorial Day. Flowers are suitable for the springtime. The pumpkins and corn and autumn leaves are suitable for the fall season. In midwinter there are few flowers, so it is most natural that the evergreens should be used to decorate the home. Surely God is not displeased if we pay attention to some of His natural beauties.

But the decorations on a Christmas tree could not possibly be called heathen, could not possibly have any idolatrous significance. Who thinks that heathen people worshiped their gods with paper chains? Who thinks that popcorn on a string is a form of idolatry? Who thinks that electric lights on a tree, for the joy of little children and to brighten the home while people sing Christmas carols, are sinful? I love Christmas and Christmas decorations, and I do not think they are wrong. They are but an expression of that joy that is in the heart as I think how God became man, how the Creator became a baby, how though "he was rich, yet for your sakes he became poor, that ye through his poverty might be rich" (II Cor. 8:9).

5. Some Object to Christmas Because of Worldliness and Unchristian Revelry That Takes Place During the Holidays.

It is true that a great many people do not honor Jesus Christ at Christmas. I think they greatly sin. Some people drink more liquor during Christmastime than at any other time in the year. That is a sin. Many business people think of Christmas only as a time to make money. In this they are wrong. Sometimes even Christian people tell the silly lie about Santa Claus and deceive little children with a heathen legend, when they could tell about the dear Lord Jesus. I think that is wickedness. A lie is always wrong and always hateful to God. Deceit is the poorest possible way to honor the birth of the Lord Jesus. I do not believe in having Santa Clauses at Sunday School or church services unless everybody understands that it is only a little parody, it is only play-acting. Certainly to deceive little children with a lie about Santa Claus is a sin. No Christian ought to condone it. Here the truth is so much better than a lie. We should tell people that the dear Lord Jesus came into the world to save sinners. Yes, people often dishonor God at Christmas. I am sorry they do. I hope no Christian who reads this will grieve God by such sins.

But we should not turn Christmas over to Satan and wicked people because some sin at Christmas.

Should we abandon Sunday because it is often misused? On the Lord's day there is more drunkenness than on any other day of the week. There is more revelry. Should Christians, therefore, count the Lord's day the Devil's day and give it up? Certainly not! There are a great many people who teach that baptism is essential to salvation. They give more honor to the water than to the blood of Christ. That is wrong. But should we, therefore, disobey Jesus Christ about baptism because some others have overstressed baptism and made it a false doctrine?

The second coming of Christ has been a greatly-abused and perverted doctrine with many. False cults have greatly perverted the doctrine of Christ's coming. People set dates. They speculate on signs. Should the rest of us honest Bible Christians, then, ignore the clear Bible doctrine of Christ's imminent second coming because the doctrine has been abused? Certainly not!

Nor should we ignore the Bible doctrine of the fullness of the Spirit because many people associate it with talking in tongues and with sinless perfection.

Just so, we would be very foolish if we turned Christmas over to Satan and worldlings. If the world has a Christmas of revelry, let us make it a day of Christian love and fellowship and a day honoring to Christ. Let us make much of the Christmas story in the Bible, of Christmas carols, of Christian love and fellowship.

Do other people make giving of gifts a mere form? Well, it does not need to be so for Christians. Christians can give gifts that really express love. They can make the gifts the response of an honest heart. We can send greetings with Scripture verses and with holy admonitions on them.

Is it wrong to have a day of rejoicing? Is it wrong to feast and to send portions to others? No indeed! When the remnant of Israel went back to the land of promise from the captivity in Babylon, under Nehemiah, the law was read and explained, and the people wept. But it was not a time for weeping, but a time for rejoicing. The wall of Jerusalem had been rebuilt. The gates had been hung. The city had been restored as the city of God, and the worship had begun. So let us listen to the plain commands of the Lord in such a case, as given in Nehe-miah 8:9, 10:

> *"And Nehemiah, which is the Tirshatha, and Ezra the priest the scribe, and the Levites that taught the people, said unto all the people, This day is holy unto the Lord your God; mourn not, nor weep. For all the people wept, when they heard the words of the law. Then he said unto them, Go your way, eat the fat, and drink the sweet, and send portions unto them for whom nothing is prepared: for this day is holy unto our Lord: neither be ye sorry; for the joy of the Lord is your strength."*

And we are glad to learn in verse 12 below:

> *"And all the people went their way to eat, and to drink, and to send portions, and to make great mirth, because they had understood the words that were declared unto them."*

If Israelites would honor God by having a day of joy and feasting and of sending portions to others because the wall was rebuilt, and the gates were set up, and the worship established, then Christian people today do well to have a day of rejoicing over the birth of the Saviour and to send portions to one another and to make merry with spiritual joy!

9

Yes, I love Christmas! I feel near to God at Christ-mas-time. I love the Word of God at Christmas. We read it and quote it again and again at our house. I like to use the Christmas time as a good excuse to get into people's hearts and win them to Christ. And, thank God, many have been saved because I brought a Christmas message, or because I urged sinners to accept God's great Christmas gift at Christmastime.

Let us have, then, a happy Christmas, and make Christ supreme on this day which we remember in honor of His birth!

The Shepherds' Christmas

"And there were in the same country shepherds abiding in the field, keeping watch over their flock by night. And, lo, the angel of the Lord came upon them, and the glory of the Lord shone round about them: and they were sore afraid. And the angel said unto them, Fear not: for, behold, I bring you good tidings of great joy, which shall be to all people. For unto you is born this day in the city of David a Saviour, which is Christ the Lord. And this shall be a sign unto you; Ye shall find the babe wrapped in swaddling clothes, lying in a manger. And suddenly there was with the angel a multitude of the heavenly host praising God, and saying, Glory to God in the highest, and on earth peace, good will toward men. And it came to pass, as the angels were gone away from them into heaven, the shepherds said one to another, Let us now go even unto Bethlehem, and see this thing which is come to pass, which the Lord hath made known unto us. And they came with haste, and found Mary, and Joseph, and the babe lying in a manger. And when they had seen it, they made known abroad the saying which was told them concerning this child. And all they that heard it wondered at those things which were told them by the shepherds. But Mary kept all these things, and pondered them in her heart. And the shepherds returned, glorifying and praising God for all the things that they had heard and seen, as it was told unto them."—Luke 2:8–20.

THE CHRISTMAS story so takes hold on my heart each year that I want to preach about it even into January! I want to preach about the wise men, about the believing virgin, about faithful Joseph, about the prophecies fulfilled in Christ's coming, about the annunciation, about there being no room in the inn, about the stable birth and the manger bed. Who could ever finish preaching about the Christmas story! But in this message let us turn aside and enjoy the first Christmas with the shepherds watching their flocks in the fields that night when the angel of the Lord brought to them the message of the Saviour! Let us hear the message and follow them as they go to see for themselves the Baby Jesus and go away with great joy!

I. The Shepherds

"And there were in the same country shepherds abiding in the field, keeping watch over their flock by night."—Luke 2:8.

Things went their humdrum way at Rome, the center of the world. In Caesar's palace the entertainment, the feasting, the politics continued; no one knew that God had a Son born, and man a Saviour! That night the head of Caesar rested as uneasily as ever rests the head that wears a crown. The Roman Senate never saw an angel come, never heard a whisper of the Glory to God in the highest chorus. They never dreamed in Rome that the King of the Jews was born who will one day rule the whole world.

In the king's palace at Jerusalem, murderous Herod had no thought that only six miles away one was born who will one day make Jerusalem the joy of the whole earth and there will establish His reign forever on David's throne! The Sanhedrin met as usual; the scribes,

12

Pharisees and Sadducees quarreled about the details of the ceremonial law. None of them had an inkling that the Christ, the Messiah so long promised, had been born. God did not think it worthwhile to tell the story of the Saviour's birth in the palaces, or universities, or among the rich and mighty of world. When Jesus was born, the angel of the Lord left Heaven, sought out a group of humble shepherds, and told to them the story that should have electrified the world!

Not until the wise men from the East came seeking "the king of the Jews" and inquired of Herod and he of the scibes, did the "powers that be," in Jerusalem, hear that a Saviour had been born!

A Saviour for the lowly, the ignorant, and the poor! This, surely, is the meaning of this Scripture.

The rich have more money to spend for Christmas. They think they can bring happiness to their loved ones by giving diamonds, or automobiles, or other costly and beautiful gifts. But these things do not make Christmas. What makes Christmas is to have the Saviour. Thank God, the poor may have Him as readily as the rich! The ignorant, the unlearned, the unsophisticated, the lower strata of society— the Saviour's birth was for such as these.

We were very poor at Christmastime during my boyhood in west Texas. One Christmas my father was deeply distressed because he felt he could not give his children the things that would make them happy. In desperation, after he saw us hang up our stockings in childish faith, notwithstanding his solemn warnings that there would be no gifts, my father pondered what to do. Then when we were all in bed he went out in the night, woke up the owner of the general merchandise store, and bought on credit the oranges, nuts, candy, and a five-cent package of firecrackers for every child's stocking. A blessed memory it is of his love and devotion. But he need not have put so much stress on these outward things. Thank God, Christmas was there in our hearts. We knew the Christmas story and the song of the angels. And the story of the virgin mother and her Holy Child is as sweet in a bare cottage as in a palace. When will we learn that God has His very best for the poor and the weak of the world!

So the angel of the Lord came to the shepherds that night and there told his wondrous story.

It is well for us to remember that our Saviour was born into a home of poverty. Joseph and Mary were undistinguished. Though both were of royal lineage, distantly, they had neither money nor standing that could gain them a room in the crowded inn. Mary must have been well content with a bed of straw. Her innocent babe was wrapped in swaddling clothes, not in a beautifully stitched and expensive layette. If the Baby Jesus heard the ox munching hay, or saw in the flickering light of a candle the stable walls, or was pricked by the rough straw, He need not have been, and I am sure was not, surprised. For He had come into a world as the humblest and weakest. Later He was to say to a prospective disciple, "The foxes have holes, and the birds of the air have nests; but the Son of man hath not where to lay his head" (Matt. 8:20).

In this same second chapter of Luke we find how the Baby Jesus was presented in the Temple. Mary brought a sacrifice, an offering, and she must needs be content to give the sacrifice which the very poorest people give, "a pair of turtledoves, or two young pigeons." I say, Jesus was born into poverty.

He lived in obscurity in Nazareth, one of the least-known towns of Galilee, until He was thirty years old. His custom was to labor there in the carpenter shop.

Blessed plan of God, which provided a Saviour for the meek and lowly in heart, for those who labor and are heavy laden! He who is personified Wisdom was called by the Pharisees unlearned! He who is Creator, God Almighty come in human form, was accused of being possessed of devils! He who had all the wealth of the world in His hands, as the Creator and Sustainer of all things, died with only one seamless garment as His estate, died between two thieves and was buried in a borrowed grave!

When Jesus told the parable of the great supper, that supper when the Father makes a wedding feast for His Son, to which all men are invited, no wonder He had the master say to his servant, "Go out quickly into the streets and lanes of the city, and bring in hither the poor, and the maimed, and the halt, and the blind" (Luke14:21). No wonder we are told, "The common people heard him gladly" (Mark 12:37). No wonder publicans and harlots, fishermen and farmers, beggars and lepers, thronged about Him. No wonder a fallen girl could weep over His feet, or that a woman, twelve years with an issue of blood, could timidly reach down and touch the hem of His garment, or that the afflicted could challenge Him boldly, "Lord, if thou wilt, thou canst make me clean" (Matt. 8:2; Luke 5:12). So when the angel came to tell of the Saviour's birth, he was sent to poor, unlearned and humble shepherds in a field watching their flocks.

Hear this, laboring people! Hear this, poor people, ignorant people, little children! Jesus came to the meek and lowly in heart.

Are there rich people who would come to Jesus? Then

they must be poor in spirit if they would see Him. Are there famous and learned and important people who would come to Jesus and find a Saviour? Then they must humble themselves like a little child, for "except ye be converted, and become as little children, ye shall not enter into the kingdom of heaven" (Matt. 18:3). Are there virtuous, moral people who are well content with themselves for their righteousness, their church membership, their ceremonial rites, or their good deeds? Then they will never get to Jesus except they come like the poor publican, saying, "God be merciful to me a sinner" (Luke 18:13). Jesus is meek and lowly in heart.

Let this Christmastime, then, be a happy time for all who are poor, or weak, or sinful, or in trouble, for the Saviour was born just for such as you, and the proof is this: the angel of the Lord was sent to announce the birth to these same shepherds in the fields watching their flocks by night!

II. The Angels

"And, lo, the angel of the Lord came upon them, and the glory of the Lord shone round about them: and they were sore afraid. And suddenly there was with the angel a multitude of the heavenly host praising God."—Luke 2:9,13.

First there was one particular angel, the angel of the Lord. Perhaps it was the same Angel Gabriel who announced the conception to Mary, the same angel of the Lord who appeared to Joseph in a dream. Then the heavenly host appeared with him.

People who do not believe in angels can have no Christmas! The angel of the Lord was a miraculous being, a wonder-worker, bringing a message from God Himself.

16

The Bible is a book of angels, because it is a book of the supernatural. No angels—no Saviour! No angels—no Gospel! No angels—no Christianity! Those who do not believe in angels do not believe in the virgin birth, do not believe in the atoning blood, do not believe in the inspired Bible. And Christmas is not worth having without all these.

Modernists really have no Christmas, in the Bible sense. When you have Jesus born as only the son of Joseph and Mary, without any divine predictions; when you have Him live a life with no miracles; when you have Him die the death of a martyr but not risen bodily from the grave, not ascend up to Heaven,—then you do not have Christianity! Christianity is a supernatural religion. Anybody who believes in Christ can believe that the angels came to announce His birth. Those who deny the angels deny the purity of the Lord's mother and make her a fallen Jewish girl and Jesus a illegitimate child. Those who do not believe in the angels make the Bible a human book, full of myths and legends and folklore and mistakes; a very good book, to be sure, but not nearly so good, the modernists and infidels think, as they themselves could write! We had as well accept this fact at the very beginning: the birth of Christ is not worth celebrating unless we accept the implications of all the supernatural that attended His birth.

No, if Jesus is a Saviour at all, then all the miracles in connection with His birth and life and death and resurrection and ascension are easily credible. I believe in the divine predictions of the coming Saviour's birth. I believe in His virgin conception and virgin birth without a human father. I believe in His perfect life, His atoning, substitutionary death, His resurrection from the grave. I believe He ascended to Heaven bodily that and that He is coming again the same way. Hence I believe in the angels. The angel of the Lord, who announced those "good tidings of great joy, which shall be to all people", is as historically credible as Christopher Columbus or George Washington or Abraham Lincoln. That heavenly host who appeared in the bright light, which was the glory of the Lord, is as real to me as the choir of three hundred voices that sang the Hallelujah Chorus in my great revival campaign in Buffalo, New York, in 1944.

Angels? Why certainly there were angels when the Saviour was born.

In every household across the land, and in every land where they really celebrate Christmas, there is a sense of growing expectancy as Christmastime draws near. Weeks before Christmas my office force is helping me type the names for my Christmas letter. I ponder: what shall I get for my wife? for Grace? for Mary? for Elizabeth? for Jessie Ruth? for Joanna? for Sarah Joy? for my office workers? Months ahead of time I plan my preaching schedule so as to be home for Christmas. Once when I got home Christmas day the Christmas tree and all the presents were left intact until Daddy arrived. I plan copy for the Christmas issue of the SWORD OF THE LORD ahead of time. Stores get out their decorations; Christmas stock is bought months in advance. What a stir of preparation as Christmas draws nigh!

Can you imagine, then, how the angelic hosts prepared for the first Christmas? Before the world began, Christ Himself and the Father had planned for it. Centuries past, prophets had been inspired to write of it. Moses, Isaiah, David, all knew of His coming in advance, and Isaiah had promised that He should be born of a virgin (Isa. 7:14). Micah had said He must be born in Bethlehem (Mic. 5:2). God had brought it about that some time before the emperor at Rome had decreed that everybody should go back to his ancestral home to be registered for taxation. The emperor little dreamed that this was only a preparation for the first Christmas, that God Himself would fulfill His promises, and that the Saviour would be born in Bethlehem.

I think that the angels entered into this glad secret more joyfully than anybody ever helped to trim a Christmas tree, or made paper chains, or strung cranberries and popcorn, or wrapped packages, or cooked a turkey or fruit cake, or packed little stockings, or lighted the candles!

How the angels must have rejoiced as the day drew nigh. I think there was a holy competition among them. All the angles in Heaven must have gathered to watch, unseen, as Gabriel made himself known to that pure, sweet, virgin girl, Mary and told her that she was to become the mother of the Saviour! Poor, troubled Joseph went about his duties with a troubled, sad heart. Who would ever have thought that of Mary? Mary, the pure, the sweet, the innocent!—and now to have a child out of wedlock. How could it ever have come about that Mary should fall into sin! So he must have mused when he found that Mary was to have a child. The angels knew the secret. And once when troubled Joseph lay in sleep God sent an angel to reveal to him, "Joseph, thou son of David, fear not to take unto thee Mary thy wife: for that which is conceived in her is of the Holy Ghost. And shall bring forth a son, and thou shalt call his name JESUS: for he shall save his people from their sins" (Matt.1:20,21). How the angels rejoiced in that! I can imagine that every angel and cherub in Heaven hugged themselves joy. They could hardly keep the secret from the human race, the ones to whom they ministered, these frail human beings of whom the angels are the guardians and ministers!

Why, the angels must have been listening in with dear Simeon, that just and devout man, when "it was revealed unto him by the Holy Ghost, that he should not see death, before he had seen the Lord's Christ" (Luke 2:26). I think heavenly hosts of angels gathered around to set the star on its journey, the star which was seen of the wise men in East; and many angels, no doubt, encamped around about these wise men who feared God and delivered them on their journey to the place where the Saviour would be found.

An angel appeared to Zacharias and promised the birth of John the Baptist, the forerunner, who was born six months before Jesus. Why, it seems angels had much to do with almost everything concerning the birth of the Saviour. It is no surprise, then, that the angels ministered to Christ in the Garden of Gethsemane; that angels stood by the open sepulcher or sat upon the stone which one had rolled away from the door. It is no surprise that when Jesus ascended into Heaven and the disciples gazed after Him with awe, "two men stood by them in white apparel [angels]; Which also said, Ye men of Galilee, why stand ye gazing up into heaven? this same Jesus, which is taken up from you into heaven, shall so come in like manner as ye have seen him go into heaven" (Acts 1:10,11).

Certainly angels had to be at the birth of Christ. It would have been a strange Christmas with no angels!

Could there be jealousy among the angels? I think not, among those sinless and lovely beings who are the ministers of the heirs of salvation, those who walk into the presence of a holy God unashamed. But it seems that every angel of God must have wanted to do something, to have some small part in announcing the birth of the Saviour.

When his team has almost won a game safely, a good football coach often sends in all the substitutes who have worked hard, so they can earn their letters, and everybody has a chance to play. Sunday School teachers, putting on a Children's Day program, try to find something that every child can do. So I think God made every angel of the universe happy by letting them join that heavenly host who shouted, "Glory to God in the highest, and on earth peace, good will toward men!"

So the glad event was announced, and I think that the angels went back about their duties happier for having announced to the shepherds that a Saviour had come, than they would have been to direct a flaming comet across the sky or to change the tides or seasons or set a new sun in the universe!

All true believers, little children in whose heart faith comes so easily, older and harder hearts who find the world too much with us and our ears too dim to hear, our eyes too nearsighted to see holy things, will be wise this Christmas if we listen ever so closely and see if we can hear again an angel speaking the message, "For unto you is born this day in the city of David a Saviour, which is Christ the Lord"! It will be a sweet Christmas if we can hear faintly the angelic host proclaiming, "Glory to God in the highest," and announcing, "Peace on earth, good will toward men." Oh, may our poor human eyes this Christmastime see a little of the glory of the Lord shine round about us! What is a Christmas without angels and the glory of the Lord?

III. The Message

"And the angel said unto them, Fear not: for, behold, I bring you good tidings of great joy, which shall be to all people. For unto you is born this day in the city of David a Saviour, which is Christ the Lord. Glory to God in the highest and on earth peace, good will toward men"— Luke 2:10,11,14.

"Fear not," said the angel. The shepherds were sore afraid, but they need not have been. Angels seem to love men with a holy love. They guard us, deliver us, report back to Heaven about us, are intensely interested in all we do. This angel surely loved these shepherds and wished them well. He came to bring them good tidings; so he said to the frightened men, "Fear not".

When Zacharias saw the angel who came to announce to him in the temple the coming birth of John the Baptist, "he was troubled, and fear fell upon him", but when the angel came to Joseph in a dream to announce the birth of Jesus, he said, "Fear not to take unto thee Mary thy wife". Even Mary, blessed, blessed Mary, most blessed among women, who had sought and found favor with God, "when she saw him [the angel], she was troubled at his saying." But again, the angel said unto her, "Fear not, Mary." Angels are always having to tell men not to be afraid. What a pitiful commentary upon a sinning race of mankind, so alien to Heaven and heavenly beings, so far from God and hence so uneasy at the presence of any of God's messengers that we are always afraid when angels appear! And what an example of the unfailing, benevolent loving-kindness of God, that always when angels come they speak to take away our fears, to comfort our hearts, to bring us good news. At least it was so about these angels who came to announce the birth of Christ.

Fear not, you shepherds in the fields outside Bethlehem! You need not be afraid of this angel, for he brings the best news ever brought to mankind. Fear not, you shepherds, for this angel brings such news as will make it so you will need never be afraid any more. You need not be afraid of death, for you can know that death will only usher you into the presence of God and an eternal joy. You need not be afraid of damnation, the natural and proper and righteous judgment on sin, if you will repent and be saved, for Jesus Himself will take our sins on Himself and pay for them all, and we can walk into the presence of God unashamed and unafraid, knowing our sins are forgiven, our hearts are made white, our record made clear.

During war, mothers have hearts that grow sick in the night as they long, with unspeakable forebodings, to hear from their boys. Widows and wives and brides-to-be with sweethearts on the other side of the sea, wait with a numbness of spirit, when it seems that all of life stands still until war be over, and fear grips their hearts. I have seen the haunted faces of these girls, when two, three months went by without a letter, and then their ecstacy and joy when word came at last that the loved one was safe.

Oh, fear is in millions of hearts today for one reason or another. I want to say to you on the authority of this angel of God, Fear not! God can take away the fear. We have a Saviour who loved us enough to leave Heaven and its glory and live among men, die a sinner's death, and rise from the dead. And if God gave His Son, He will give anything else we need to those of us who trust Him. "He that spared not his own Son, but delivered him up for us all, how shall he not with him also freely give us all things?" (Rom. 8:32).

There are people who are never wakened by a phone call in the middle of the night, are never handed a telegram, never called by long distance, but that a startled fear sweeps over their spirit. Fear is a terrible thing. Blessed be God, we have a Saviour who means an end to fear in those who trust Him. "Perfect love casteth out fear"(I John 4:18).

"Tidings of great joy, which shall be to all people". Good news for everybody!

Dear reader, I beg you to enjoy your part of the Christmas joy. I am not speaking of the pleasures some seek at Christmastime. I speak not of the sensate pleasures and the fleshly enjoyments of the dance, nor the excited flush that drink will bring to many at Christmastime. There is a better joy than that.

I am not speaking now even of those holy joys of the family and home and love expressed in gifts and greetings. I hope everyone who reads these lines will have home and love and what comfort loved ones bring at Christmastime. This is closer to my heart than most people can ever know, because I am a traveler, a stranger and wanderer on the face of the earth, gone out about the Lord's business most of the time and returning only briefly to those I love the best. I say, I hope all of you have whatever proper joy comes from giving and receiving presents, from greetings and letters, and from mother's cooking or that of your wife. I hope you hear the glad cries of little children as they empty their stockings and unwrap their presents. I hope you join in the Christmas carols and gaze at the lighted Christmas tree and chat with the relatives you haven't seen for many long months. I want you to have these good joys. But God has better joy for you than that, my friend!

"For unto you is born this day in the city of David a Saviour," said the angels. Ah, a Saviour! That is the best news anybody ever heard!

I looked in the sad face of a man behind bars, a man condemned to die. He did not need a good teacher. He needed pardon, forgiveness, salvation. He needed a Saviour! Jesus is a teacher, but He is more than that. He is a physician, but He is more than that. No prophet or sage ever spoke as Jesus spoke. No life was ever as holy or pure. No example ever shone as bright across the path of youth. But O, beloved readers, let us remember this: Christ is nothing to us until He is first of all a Saviour! People who talk the foolish talk of a social gospel, by which they mean labor unions, and relief projects, and social security, do not really know anything about Christmas! Men do not really need the soup and soap most. When they get a Saviour, the by-products of the Gospel will transform their lives. If you want to cure the evils of a slum district, get people converted. Soon they will be out of the slums, and into better jobs. If you want to get people educated, then get them truly saved, and lights will beckon them they never before knew existed, and ideals and ambitions will arise that grow naturally out of the Gospel's fruit. It is silly to talk about doing much to help mankind until you get mankind to come to Jesus Christ.

Foolish America does not remember that nearly all of our great colleges and universities were founded by preachers, founded with Christian motives. Wesley's revival saved England from a French Revolution. D. L. Moody did more to change America from a half-civilized backwoods than all the presidents we have ever elected.

What mankind needs is a Saviour. The by-products of Christianity bring civilization. And, thank God, a Saviour is what we have in Jesus.

You may go and tell people that if they want to have a real Christmas they need to learn what it is to have forgiveness of sins, to have their poor souls saved, to make sure of a home in Heaven.

Dear sinner, you can never enjoy Christmas as I enjoy it and as millions of others do, until you can look up into the Father's face and tell Him that you have received His Christmas Gift, that you have the joy He promised by the angels that first Christmas night! It is silly, it is dishonest, it is wicked, it is tragic to try to celebrate Christmas without accepting Christ as Saviour.

Look in the show windows. Every store that puts up Christmas mottoes is but the business of a hypocrite if the owner himself does not know Jesus as a Saviour. "Merry Christmas!" you cry, but not in any real sense can you know the merry heart of Christmas until you have the load of sin lifted off of it and know that you have a Saviour.

Christmas will mean disillusionment, disappointment, an aching head, money wasted, and worse, for many a soul who has not let Jesus come in to be the joy of Christmas, to be what He came to be—a Saviour. How can you have Christmas without accepting God's gift? If you do not accept Christ as your own Saviour, how do you know what the Saviour spoke about when He gave these tidings of great joy? The good news is for all people. It is for you. Make sure you appropriate it.

What Saviour is this that is promised? It is "Christ the Lord." The word *Christ* means "the anointed one". *Christ* or *Christos* is the Greek form; *Messiah* is the Hebrew form. The angel simply meant to say that the promised Messiah of the Old Testament is the Saviour of the New. That Baby Jesus, born in Bethlehem, laid in a manger, is the suffering servant of Isaiah 53. He is the virgin-born Son of Isaiah 7:14. He is the one whose "name shall be called Wonderful, Counsellor, The mighty God, The everlasting Father, The Prince of Peace" (Isa. 9:6). He is the great seed of David who will sit on David's throne, often foretold. He is the "anointed" of Psalm 2:2, the "Son" of Psalm 2:12. He is the Prophet whom Moses foretold in Deuteronomy 18:15. He is the Seed of Abraham mentioned in Genesis 13:15, 16 and Genesis 17:6–8. This Baby Jesus is the Holy One David foresaw should never see corruption in the grave (Ps. 16:10) but should rise again. He is the crucified One whose heart is revealed in Psalm 22. Jesus is the Christ of the Old Testament.

This angel there authenticated all the Old Testament as the Word of God, and if Jesus is not the one foretold to come, then He was no more than other men. If Christ stands as the Son of God, then the Bible stands as the Word of God.

"Christ the Lord" is the name of the Saviour. The word *Lord* attests His deity. It is a word which is used about God, but Christ was not ashamed to claim it, for He too is God, come in human form. He is the Son of the Almighty, but one of His names, too, is "The mighty God" (Isa. 9:6).

The Creator of the heavens and the earth has been born of a woman, has nursed at a mother's breast, has grown to manhood in perfection, has died an atoning death on the cross for man's sin! This is the Saviour who was announced by the angels that night in the fields outside Bethlehem. "For unto you is born this day in the city of David a Saviour, which is Christ the Lord."

And my heart runs over with joy as I thank God that this Saviour is *my Saviour.*

"Unto you is born..."Unto *me* is born a Saviour. He is *mine.* One day I gave myself to Him, and He gave Himself to me. My sins are forgiven. My soul is saved. He is my own Saviour, praise God! I pray that He is yours, too, dear reader. And if you have not taken Him as your Saviour, do it this moment. By simple faith reach out and claim Him.

"Glory to God in the highest, and on earth peace, good will toward men," chanted the heavenly hosts. Then Christ is the glory of the Father—Christ alone of all that were ever born, perfectly fulfills the Father's will. And as He is the glory of the Father, so is He the hope of all mankind. There will never be any peace on earth except that which brings glory to God.

Peace is a wonderful gift. Do you have peace?

One November night in Dallas, Texas, I lay sick with the flu. The telephone rang, and when Mrs. Rice answered I heard her say, I am sorry, but Mr. Rice is sick in bed with the flu. I am sure he would be glad to see you if it were not for that."

"What is it, Mother?" I called.

She answered, "A couple wanted to come and have you pray for them. I told them you are sick in bed and could not get up to see them."

"Tell them if they will come back to my bedroom I will be glad to pray for them," I said.

I heard her tell the unknown inquirer over the telehone and learned that they promised to come at once to my home.

They came. One was a man who, the second day before, had locked himself in a hotel room and turned on the gas at the unlighted room heater. His home was broken, his health was gone. It was in the heart of the depression, and he had nowhere to go—no job, no money, no food. So he decided to end it all. The woman who was with him was a hotel chambermaid who smelled the gas, unlocked the door, opened the windows, called the ambulance, and saved his life. The two had been drawn together by the incident. He had told the woman his sad life, and she had told him of her fall and life of shame. That Saturday night they walked the streets, disconsolate, troubled. Both had come alike, it seemed, to the end of everything good and happy. Brokenly, he suggested "We need somebody to pray for us. Let's go to the priest's house and ask him to pray for us."

They went to the house of the priest and knocked at the door. It was late at night, but the troubled man said, "Father, we are in trouble and sin. We came to ask you to pray for us."

The priest said to them sharply, "I dare say both of you have been drinking, and here you come to my door to disturb me at night when I have a mass at 6:00 in the morning! Get away from my door!"

They turned away, sadder than ever. But the woman thought of her mother, and said, "I'll bet my mother's pastor would pray for us. He wouldn't talk to anybody that way. Let's go and ask Brother Rice to pray for us."

He refused, saying, "I have been run away from one man's house tonight. I won't go, unless you first call and find out if he is willing to pray for us."

So they telephoned, and then when I asked them to come, they came to my home.

I often look into the faces of despair: of men in jail, of sot drunkards who come into the missions to get out of the cold and for a cup of coffee, girls who come to ask what they can do to avoid public shame after their sin, people with broken homes and broken hearts. But I think I never saw two sadder faces than those two who were led by my wife into my bedroom that November night in Dallas, Texas!

I sat up in bed and told them I was glad they had come, that God loved them, that I loved them too. I told them if they would kneel down beside my bed, the best I could I would ask the Lord to forgive their sins and come into their hearts and show them how to have peace and joy again. They knelt. They were unashamed of their tears. I had tears, too. I put my hands upon their heads and prayed. The angels stooped to listen as they sobbed in penitence over ruined and wasted lives, and as I prayed and wept over two sinners who, just as all of us do, needed mercy, though they did not deserve it. As they knelt there I told them how to trust the Saviour; how to trust Him for salvation now and for victory tomorrow. After a season they arose and sat beside the bed. There were many problems, many questions to be answered. I helped them the best I could with the Word of God.

After a bit, that poor man, with shabby clothes, who came out of the night to ask me to pray for him, looked it me intently and said, "Preacher, this is the strangest thing I ever said!"

"What is strange?" I asked.

"Why, day before yesterday I tried to kill myself. I didn't want to live. I didn't have anything to live for. We have walked up and down the streets all afternoon and this evening, trying to find what to do. I was never in such a turmoil and trouble of mind and heart in my life as I have been just today and yesterday. And now someway, strangely, it is all gone. I am not worried. I am not unhappy. I don't have any anxiety about a job or about what will happen to me tomorrow. I just feel the quietest peace in here," he said, and he tapped himself over his heart. "Isn't that strange?" he asked.

"That is not strange," I said. "I have seen the same thing happen to thousands of others. Peace is what Jesus gives. Nobody in the world can ever have true peace without coming to take Jesus as Saviour. He is our peace."

That blustery November night that poor ruined man learned what the angels meant when they sang, "Glory to God in the highest, and on earth peace, good will toward men." Oh, may the peace of Jesus this Christmas be with you who read this!

IV. The Experience

We have talked about the shepherds, the angels, the angels' message, and it would be a lovely story if the story ended there. But it does not. The shepherds did not have to leave the matter with a sweet message from Heaven, but no practical results in their lives. Listen to the rest of the story.

"And it came to pass, as the angels were gone away from them into heaven, the shepherds said one to another, Let us now go even unto Bethlehem, and see this thing which is come to pass, which the Lord hath made known unto us. And they came with haste, and found Mary, and Joseph, and the babe lying in a manger. And when they had seen it, they made known abroad the saying which was told them concerning this child. And all they that heard it wondered at those things which were told them by the shepherds. But Mary kept all these things, and

pondered them in her heart. And the shepherds returned, glorifying and praising God for all the things that they had heard and seen, as it was told unto them."—Luke 2:15–20.

First, these shepherds believed the story. They said, "Let us now go even unto Bethlehem, and see this thing which is come to pass." Blessed, thrice blessed, are they who believe the Word of God! Remember that Jesus Himself said later, after His resurrection, to the doubting disciples, "O fools, and slow of heart to believe all that the prophets have spoken" (Luke 24:25). These shepherds were ignorant, but they believed the words of the angel, the message sent from Heaven! And in my heart at this Christmas season I praise the Lord for millions of common people who still believe all the story of the Babe who was born in Bethlehem, believe that the angels really appeared, that the Glory of God shone round about, that Jesus was born of the Virgin Mary as the Scripture says. Other people may have believed after they went to see, but the shepherds believed before they went! Doubting Thomas missed the first appearance of Jesus after His resurrection, and would not believe the disciples. He said, "Except I shall see in his hands the print of the nails, and put my finger into the print of the nails, and thrust my hand into his side, I will not believe" (John 20:25). When Jesus appeared again and Thomas saw Him and was convinced, he said, "My Lord and my God." Hear, then, the answer of Jesus, "Thomas, because thou hast seen me, thou has believed: blessed are they that have not seen, and yet have believed." Sin is back of all the unbelief about the Lord Jesus Christ and the Bible and God's revelation about salvation. One reason the angels brought the message to these shepherds is that they knew the shepherds would believe it.

Second, these honest-hearted shepherds made an honest investigation. They really wanted to see the Lord Jesus who was born at Bethlehem and wrapped in swaddling clothes and laid in a manger. "And they came with haste, and found Mary, and Joseph, and the babe lying in a manger" (Luke 2:16). Oh, this Christmastime, how blessed it would be if every unbeliever, every infidel, every agnostic and doubter, would only give God a chance to prove Himself!

The Baby was there! They had a chance to see for themselves that the angel's message was true! So did doubting Thomas, who said he would believe if he could see the nailprints and put his hand in the nailprints and in the wounded side of the Saviour. He really got a chance to prove to himself that Jesus was risen from the dead. So it was that Nathaniel, who did not believe that any good thing could come out of Nazareth, finally obeyed the urging of his friend, Philip, and came to see. And Nathaniel said, "Rabbi, thou art the Son of God; thou art the King; of Israel (John 1:49). The Queen of Sheba did not believe all the wondrous things that were told about the divinely given wisdom of Solomon. But her honest heart at least led her to come and see, and she learned "that the half was not told me!"

Here is a principle of God's loving mercy: a hungry heart always can find out the truth about God if it wants to. Always a doubting soul, who really wants to know, can find out whether the Bible is true, whether Christ is the Son of God, whether the Bible will work in a modern world. Remember that Jesus said in John 7:17, "If any man will do his will, he shall know of the doctrine, whether it be God, or whether I speak of myself." This means *would be,* if any man be willing to do his will, he shall know that those who really seek God with a willing heart will find Him.

That was the very same principle stated in Jeremiah 29:13, "And ye shall seek me, and find me, when ye shall search for me with all your heart."

The same kind of promise is in Hosea 6:3, "Then shall we know, if we follow on to know the Lord."

Blessed promises these which show that any doubter, any distressed and darkened mind, any troubled but honestly seeking heart can find the Saviour! Those shepherds went to see the Baby Jesus. How simple, how wise, how blessed that was!

Too many people sit out in the field in the darkened night and say, "I do not believe that any Baby was born of a virgin in Bethlehem. I do not believe what the angels promised. I do not believe that Jesus is a Saviour. I do not believe that He brings good news, glad tidings of great joy, which shall be to all people." Well, as long as you sit out in the field and do not go to the manger to see for yourself, you only prove the stubbornness of your self-will and the sinfulness of your heart that does not want a Saviour. These shepherds *wanted* a Saviour. They were *glad* that Jesus was born. So they went, and straightway, and with glad, believing hearts; and all their expectations were met!

Why, that is the same way the wise men came from the East! They came in glad expectancy. They came with treasures all ready to give. They were willing to follow the Word of God, as far as it led, and then they rejoiced when they saw that the star backed up the Word of God. And how glad they were when they saw the Baby Jesus and opened up their treasures and gave

Him gold and frankincense and myrrh!

Simeon in the temple had no trouble believing that Christ was Messiah, the virgin-born Son of God. Anna the prophetess who waited there had no trouble believing it. Why, down through the centuries all the humble hearts who long for God, who want forgiveness, who confess their need of a Saviour, have found no trouble believing the story of the Lord Jesus Christ, born in Bethlehem, laid in a manger, wrapped in swaddling clothes. Here is the heart of Christmas and the heart of Christianity itself! And all those who do not believe have only themselves to blame. God is ready to reveal Himself to all those who seek Him.

This Bible claims to be the Word of God. Yet I have faced infidels and so-called agnostics up and down the land and have found they were ignorant of the Bible, though it is acknowledged as the greatest book of the world, the greatest book of history, and of literature, and of morals, and humanities, even if it were not the inspired Word of God. But infidels hate the Bible, mock it, do not learn it, do not submit themselves to it.

What infidel or agnostic or boasted doubter ever spends any time in prayer, waiting on God to reveal Himself, confessing his sins, longing for forgiveness and cleansing and grace to do right? What man of all the boasted unbelievers really waits on God with a humble, contrite heart, longing for a Saviour, longing for the Truth, the Way, and the Life, and the Light?

A young man with a little learning who had been reading extracts from Tom Paine and Bob Ingersoll in those infamous little Blue Books, trashy things with paper covers selling for a nickel to the unlearned, once said to me:" I can't help it, can I, if I can't believe? I just have a scientific, investigating mind, and my reasoning does not account for God. Let those who can believe such things, do so, but a man of my background, reasoning, and investigation cannot."

However, I frankly told him that he had never made any honest investigation, never sought to find the truth about God and the Bible and Christ. I dared him, in the presence of his younger brother, to get down on his knees with me and confess to God that he was a sinner, by whatever standard he was measured, and ask that if there be a God, He make Himself known. I dared him to promise God Almighty, if there be a God, that he would honestly follow whatever light should come from God; that if the Bible proved itself the Word of God, he would obey it and love it and live by it; that if Christ proved to be the virgin-born Son of God, the only Saviour, that he would trust Him and surrender to Him as Saviour and Lord. And then I simply told the young man that I knew about God and the Bible; that I had proved it and so had his father and mother, and so had millions of other saints, and that if he, this very day, were unwilling to get down before God and humble himself and seek to find God, I would know that he was a hypocrite, unwilling to face the truth and unwilling to find it. I had him there, and he knew it. Soon he was down with me on his knees, confessing that he was frail and weak and that he had fallen short even of his own standards of morals, asking that if there be a God, He would reveal Himself to his heart; promising that he would honestly investigate the Bible and try to learn what God said, if it perchance be the Word of God. He didn't pray one minute before he was in tears, and soon he confessed that it was all true; the only trouble had been with him and not with God. God is willing to receive any seeking sinner, and to reveal Himself to any honest heart who is willing to go look into the manger and see the Baby Jesus.

Oh, wouldn't this Christmastime be the best time in the world to turn away from this folly, this idle chatter of unbelief, and make an honest investigation and see if you can find the Baby Jesus there where the Bible says He is? Why not open the Bible and begin to see whether God has a message for you, to see whether Jesus Christ does not prove Himself to be the Son of God? Why not kneel in your room before God and confess your failures and sins and shortcoming, and ask God to give you light, to show you what you ought to do? Ask God to reveal Himself! Why not face the sin question honestly (for nothing but sin ever keeps anybody from God) and confess your sins to yourself and to the Creator, wherever He be, however He may reveal Himself? Surely only a fool would say that there is no Creator. And if there be a Creator who made man, surely He cares what is in man's heart and will listen when man prays, if he pray with a humble and contrite heart, seeking the light, wanting to do right. This Christmas season, why not wait on the ministry of the Word, listen to the preaching of godly men? Why not go to some preacher who lives straight and loves men, who believes the Word of God, and with an honest heart find the truth?

Back of all infidelity is sin, defeat and self-will. I promise you that like the fog mists disappear when the sun rises and warm breezes blow, so your doubts will disappear as you wait before God, confessing your sin, reading the Bible, seeking light from Heaven. God reveals Himself to those who really seek Him with all their hearts. These humble shepherds went directly to Bethlehem, found the stable, and saw the Baby Jesus with their own eyes. They went away happy, and so may you, if you will honestly seek to know the truth this Christmas season. What a sin, what folly, and what eternal loss is yours, if you do not make Christmas your own this time by finding the Saviour for yourself!

The shepherds made haste; I hope you will do the same. This was the best news the shepherds had ever heard. It is the best news you have heard, too, and I hope you will accept it. When the prodigal son came to himself, he said, "I will arise and go to my father, and will say unto him, Father, I have sinned against heaven and before thee, And am no more worthy to be called thy son" (Luke 15:18,19). And then, bless God, he arose, and came to his father! Will you do the same today?

The last thing we will note about these shepherds is that they "returned, glorifying and praising God for all the things that they had heard and seen, as it was told unto them." Oh, then, if you have found the Lord Jesus and if you have a real Christmas in your heart, tell others about it. When a woman stooped down and touched the hem of His garment and was wonderfully healed., Jesus said, "Who touched me?" and made her stand forth and confess it (Luke 8:45–47). He wanted her to tell it. That maniac of Gadara, who had lived in the tombs, whom no man could bind, who cut himself on the stones and lived without clothes, was wonderfully converted and healed, with demons cast out. He sat at the feet of Jesus, clothed and in his right mind. He wanted to follow Jesus everywhere He went; but Jesus said to him, Return to thine own house, and shew how great things God hath done unto thee." Then we are told that "he went his way, and published throughout the whole city how great things Jesus had done unto him" (Luke 8:39).

Let us then, like the shepherds, give our glad witness the joy we have found in Jesus, with our sins forgiven and our hearts made light. Let everyone this Christmas season who knows the peace on earth the shepherds told about, and who has received as his own the Saviour then announced, tell others today and share the good news. That is what I am trying to do in this sermon.

But one thing remains to be said, and that is this. Will you accept Jesus as your own Saviour this day? This holy Christmastime, with the impulses of the Bible story, of sweet Christmas carols, and of family influences, will you be saved today? Open your heart, confess your sin to Christ, trust Him to forgive you and save you now! If you will do so, first tell the Lord so right there, then write and tell me so. You may either copy the statement which I wrote here, and sign it, giving name and address, and date, or write me in your own words as you prefer. But I beg, do it this very day! I will write you a personal letter of counsel and help and how glad I will be to do it. And be sure to tell your loved ones, too, if you take Jesus today. I mean this for unconverted sinners who will today accept Christ as Saviour.

My Decision for Christ

Date _____

Shelton L. Smith
Murfreesboro, TN
Dear Dr. Smith:

I have read Dr. Rice's sermon on "The Shepherd's Christmas". I believe the Christmas story, that Jesus was born at Bethlehem to be our Saviour. I confess myself a poor lost sinner. I believe that He died for my sins and is willing to save me now. Here and now I turn my heart to Him, I confess my sin and guilt, I depend on Him to save me! With all my heart I surrender to Him now and trust Him. I am writing this as my confession that today I take Christ as my Saviour. By His help I will try to live for Him the rest of my days.

Signed_____

Address _____

Gifts of the Wise Men

Gold—Tribute for a King

Frankincense—Worship for a God

Myrrh—Faith in a Suffering Jesus

"Now when Jesus was born in Bethlehem of Judea in the days of Herod the king, behold, there came wise men from the east to Jerusalem...And when they were come into the house, they saw the young child with Mary his mother, and fell down, and worshipped him: and when they had opened their treasures, they presented unto him gifts; gold, and frankincense, and myrrh."—Matt. 2:1,11.

THREE HUNDRED miles east of Jerusalem, across the Syrian desert, lay ancient Babylon. There, about six hundred years before Christ's birth, the Jews had been brought as captives by King Nebuchadnezzar. Daniel and three other Hebrew lads, perhaps of high school or college age, took their place after proper training and testing among the wise men, the Magi of Babylon. There Daniel rose by virtue of his character and divinely given wisdom to be successively "ruler over the whole province of Bablylon, and chief of the governors over all the wise men of Babylon" (Dan. 2:48), the third ruler of the kingdom (Dan.

5:29) under Belshazzar, and the first of three presidents over 120 princes, governing the entire worldwide kingdom (Dan. 6:1-3) under king Darius, and had great honor, evidently, under King Cyrus.

It was in Babylon that Daniel wrote the book of prophecies known by his name in our Bible. Part of the book of Daniel was written in the Chaldaic language. Daniel's prominence as a statesman under three separate dynasties of rulers, and his place as chief of the wise men, doubtless left him an enduring fame among all the learned and particularly the spiritually minded and godly wise men who followed Daniel in that ancient empire. Already the glory of world rule had departed from Babylon when Christ was born. It had been conquered first by the Medes under Darius, establishing the Media-Persian empire. Later it was conquered by Alexander the Great, then later still by the Roman legions, and Rome ruled the world in the days when Christ was born.

But in the East, still, wise men sought after God, studied the starry heavens, and doubtless pored over the ancient manuscripts of Daniel. From a study of Daniel 9:24-26, they may well have learned of the coming Prince, the Messiah or King of the Jews, who would one day bring an end to the sin and trouble of the Jews, and would be anointed the most holy King, and reign in Jerusalem. They may well have kept careful record as the years went by, sixty-nine weeks of years, or 483 years, from the time the commandment went forth in the days of Ezra and Nehemiah to rebuild Jerusalem, until the coming of the Saviour. When the sixty-nine weeks were finished, these watchers saw in the heavens—"that declare the glory of God"—a star! They took this star as a supernatural witness that the time was fulfilled, the King was born. So by faith

42

they came to Jerusalem, bringing their gifts for the new-born King. At Jerusalem they learned from the Scribes and Pharisees, who knew Micah 5:2, that the Saviour must be born in Bethlehem, a few miles distant. There they went, preceded, this last leg of the journey, by the star, and found the Baby Jesus, with His mother, Mary. Then they opened their treasures and gave gifts to the Lord Jesus Christ.

They Opened Their Treasures!

We suppose that the long, long journey these wise men had made from the East was over desert sands, through mountain passes, perhaps across the Euphrates River, as Well as the Jordan. What dangers they braved by the way, we do not know. But hidden away safely, each of them carried the things they held most dear— treasures, the best they had, reserved for the Baby King! They did not flip Him a coin of pocket change, nor hand Him casually a baby's trinket to play with. There was nothing superficial or casual in this meeting! Through long, long years their hearts had beat high with hope in anticipation of this blessed moment. They fell on their faces and worshiped Him! Then with tears of joy and with trembling lips and pulses running wild with gladness, their nervous fingers unlocked little cabinets, or unwrapped the thongs that bound their treasures, and, opening them, they gave to the Lord Jesus Christ the finest of all they had!

Some speak very blandly of the Galilean Peasant, or "Prophet of Nazareth", or the "Great Teacher", or the "Way-Shower". People call Him an example, a martyr, wise man, philosopher, prophet or seer; but such terms are but chaff to Him who deserves so much more. All such half-hearted and impersonal praise is stinking ointment instead of holy incense before Jesus. One rich man so came to Jesus, calling Him "Good Master", and He sternly reproved him, saying, "There is none good but one, that is, God" (Matt. 19:17). Jesus is more than a good schoolmaster or rabbi; if He is not God, then He is not good!

Just here every reader will do well if he probes deep into his own heart to see his attitude toward Jesus Christ. Only those who come with hearts bowed low in worship, opening all their treasures, have come as the Lord Jesus demands that men come. He Himself said, "They that worship him [the Father] must worship him in spirit and in truth" (John 4:24), and Jesus must be approached like the Father with whom He is one (John 10:30).

Many a transaction can be completed satisfactorily without opening one's treasures. One may drop a nickel for a paper, or pass a dollar to the taxi man, or buy an automobile, or rent a house, or play a game without ever revealing the things held most dear within the locked and sealed vaults where treasures are hidden. Doctors complain that patients often do not fully trust them nor reveal the details that might show what is wrong, particularly in nervous cases. Lawyers make speeches, politicians pass laws, businessmen make deals, all behind crafty eyes and poker faces, with motives hidden. And wives come weeping to tell me, sometimes, that they are shut out of their husbands' lives. Men have business dealings, have plans, amusements, friendships, hopes and aspirations, even loves, of which the wives know nothing. And, God forgive us, oftentimes in the churches, there are those who take part in religious activities and do church work, but who do not open all their treasures to the Lord Jesus Christ!

Not so with these wise men. They opened their treasures and gave gifts to the Lord Jesus Christ. And I beg you today dear reader, take Jesus Christ into the innermost secrets of your heart, lay bare your treasures, and give Him the choicest and best of everything, yea, give Him all, and rejoice that He deigns to take them.

One cannot deal with Jesus Christ as with ordinary men. One must deal with Him as God, as Creator, as One who knows all, as One who understands all, as One who loves all.

If you deal at all with Jesus Christ, you must deal sincerely. You cannot deal with Him in trifles only— rather, you must deal with Him about eternal verities of Heaven and Hell, of life and death, and sin, and salvation, and immortality. Open to Him the treasures of your heart!

You may go to church and pay your tithes, fast twice a week, pray in public, live a respectable and moral life, be loved by the poor, honored by neighbors, trusted by friends, but that does not make you a Christian. Only when the Lord Jesus Christ deals with the treasures of the innermost soul can one claim to be His.

Every gift the wise men gave had a profound meaning. It was the Spirit of God who spoke to them through the ancient prophecy of Daniel. It was the same Spirit of God who emboldened their faith by the witness of the star which they saw in the East and later over Bethlehem. The angel of the Lord guarded them and took them safely on their journey to Bethlehem, then later in a dream warned them to return another way after they had seen the Baby Jesus.

Gold, the Gift for a King

These wise men came to inquire, "Where is he that is born King of the Jews? for we have seen his star in the east, and are come to worship him" (Matt. 2:2). It is probable that from Daniel 9:25 they had read of the Messiah [or anointed] the Prince. They came, as properly they should have come, to seek a future Ruler, one born to be a king. We should never forget that Jesus was hailed at His birth as the King of the Jews. The same label was hung by Pilate on Jesus' cross when He died—"JESUS OF NAZARETH, THE KING OF THE JEWS" (John 19:19). The Prophet Isaiah had promised, "Of the increase of his government and peace there shall be no end, upon the throne of David, and upon His kingdom" (Isa. 9:7). To Mary the angel promised, "The Lord God shall give unto him the throne of his father David: And he shall reign over the house of Jacob forever; and of his kingdom there shall be no end."

When we deal with Jesus we deal with a King. And let us not explain away His kingliness by making Him simply "the King of love" or "King of hearts". The word *king* in the Bible is not used in a figurative sense. Jesus is to reign literally on this earth. For that all the Christians pray in the model prayer, if they take to heart the words they utter, "Thy kingdom come. Thy will be done in earth as it is in heaven" (Matt. 6:10). The saints in glory are pictured as saying, "We shall reign on the earth" (Rev. 5:10), and these saints, we are told, will reign with Christ a thousand years (Rev. 20:4). Christ will return to this earth to reign, crowned with many crowns, "KING OF KINGS, AND LORD OF LORDS" (Rev. 19:11–16). So the wise men, bringing gifts to the King of the Jews, brought gold.

Gold is the symbol of man's worldly possessions and is therefore fit tribute for a king. The chief priests and scribes asked the Saviour, "Is it lawful for us to give tribute unto Caesar, or no?" (Luke 20:22), but Jesus pointed to the image of Caesar and his superscription on a penny and said, "Render therefore unto Caesar the things which be Caesar's and unto God the things which be God's" (Luke 20:25). Rule and authority demand tribute. The lordship of Jesus Christ demands that He be worshiped with gifts—gifts of money and things as well as the intangible and spiritual gifts of praise and love. Since Christ is the Creator of all things and every good and perfect gift comes down from above, then to acknowledge Christ as Lord means to bring Him gifts of gold and silver and property. God put it in the hearts of these wise men from the East to bring Jesus gold as an example for all others who should ever claim to worship Jesus Christ.

Does it seem strange to you that of all the gifts here, gold is mentioned first? Why not incense first since it pictures prayer and praise, teaching the deity of Christ? Why not myrrh first since it pictures the suffering Saviour and so represents the faith that was in the believing hearts of these men who accepted Christ as their Saviour? No, according to God's plan and God's record gold was offered first. And throughout the Bible we find it true that men who sought God brought of the firstlings of their flocks, as did Abel (Gen. 4:4), or like Zacchaeus, who, converted and forgiven, I think, before he got down out of the tree, said to Jesus, "The half of my goods I give to the poor; and if I have taken any thing from any man by false accusation, I restore him fourfold" (Luke 19:8). I believe that one of the first impulses of a newly born-again soul is to give—give of money and property to the support of the work of the Lord Jesus Christ.

Cornelius, the devout Roman centurion who so earnestly sought the face of God gave alms to the poor, and this pleased the Lord so much that it is mentioned even before the statement that "he prayed to God alway" (Acts 10:2). When God sent an angel to instruct Cornelius

47

where to find Peter who would tell him how to be saved, the angel said, "Thy prayers and thine alms are come up for a memorial before God" (Acts 10:4,31).

As surely as the landlord has a right to the rent, or a banker to his interest, the Lord Jesus Christ has a right to the gold of those who claim to love and worship Him.

Preachers who talk about money are often accused of being money-minded, and any talk about giving of money and property to God is offensive to large groups of people who call themselves Christians. But there was nothing offensive in the idea of giving money to God in the mind of these wise men. When they opened their treasures, the very first thing was to take out gold. What an honor that the gold they brought could care for the needs of the little family as they fled into Egypt from the wrath of Herod! How they must have rejoiced that the first little garment the child ever wore, perhaps, was bought with the money they offered so lovingly to Jesus, their Saviour and Lord and King! How glad they must have been to support those too, who cared for Jesus. True worship involves the giving of all we have to God, and first of all our physical means.

Jesus went to church one day and, surprising as it may be to many, He "sat over against the treasury, and beheld how the people cast money into the treasury" (Mark 12:41). Jesus watched the giving of the people, talked about their giving, and drew lessons for all to hear. Any preacher who does not do the same kind of teaching is falling short of his duty and the pattern set by our Lord Jesus Christ. If you, dear reader, feel that Christian worship is wholly matter of singing and praying and things of the heart and none at all of money and material things, then you need to remember that the wise men, really wise with the spiritual wisdom given from God, gave to Jesus first gold and that Jesus Himself delighted to sit by the treasury and watch how people gave their gifts.

Too many people are willing enough for Jesus to be God and to bring Him incense of praise and prayer; too many people are willing to acknowledge Him as Saviour but are not willing to acknowledge Him as Lord and Master of all! Jesus is a King, and He has a right; He demands to exercise the right of full authority over your life, your heart, your home, your purse, and all you have. If you would come to Him in worship that is acceptable, then open your treasures and give Him all He desires. Those who give in Jesus' name, like the wise men, worship God acceptably. The gold is tribute for a king who must reign.

Frankincense—the Sweet Odor of Prayer and Praise for Deity

Frankincense was the second gift offered by the wise men to the Baby Jesus. Frankincense is mentioned in many places in the Old Testament. It was one ingredient in the sweet perfume or incense which was prepared and used only in the tabernacle and never for private or ordinary use (Exod. 30:34–38). The frankincense indicates the deity of Jesus Christ. It was to be offered in worship only to God had never to one who was simply a man. These wise men from the East, by faith and spiritual perception, recognized that Jesus, the King of the Jews, was literally the Son of God. They must have understood His virgin birth. Certainly they knew His pre-existence with God, that He was the Messiah, that He was one with the Father and worthy of all worship and praise of the whole human race! They had no silly talks about Christ as a teacher or example or good man; they instantly acknowledge that He was their God. They may never have read the promise of Isaiah 9:6 and 7, "For unto us a child is born, unto us a son is given: and the government shall be upon his shoulder: and his name shall be called...The mighty God, The everlasting Father." But the Holy Spirit who made them wise told them that Jesus was God. So they did not tickle Him under the chin nor cradle Him in their arms. They fell their faces and worshiped Him! The incense pictures the prayer and praise that is due only to God, the God who answers prayer, the God who is pure and holy and apart from sinful beings. The sweet incense including frankincense was most holy unto God. Exodus 30:37 and 38 say:

> "And as for the perfume which thou shalt make, ye not make to yourselves according to the composition thereof; it shall be unto thee holy for the Lord. Whoso-ever shall make like unto that, to smell thereto, shall even be cut off from his people."

The same Holy Spirit who inspired the Bible, taught the heart of these wise men what to bring to the Baby Jesus.

Dear reader, God is not concerned about your pious platitudes as you commend the teachings of Jesus in the sermon on the mount. He turns His face with disdain when you speak of the crucifixion as the martyrdom of a good man who died for his ideals. There is no way under Heaven that any man can approach God in peace except he come with prayer and praise to Jesus Christ as one who is very God, Creator, Saviour, one to be loved and worshiped, one who answers prayer, one who is worthy of all the praises that can fall from human lips!

There are some who study the Bible even when they should be on their knees in adoration. There are some who ask learned questions who rather should bow the knee in surrender and confession before the Lord Jesus as the Maker of Heaven and earth. The lesson the wise men would teach us is that we, like Thomas, should fall on our faces and say to Jesus, "My Lord and my God (John 20:28)."

"Whoso offereth praise glorifieth me" said God through the psalmist (Ps. 50:23). And David said, "I will bless the Lord at all times; his praise shall continually be in my mouth" (Ps. 34:1). In Psalm 65:2 the inspired address for God is, "O thou that hearest prayer, unto thee shall all flesh come." And these wise men declared plainly by their gifts that they recognized this Baby Jesus as the eternal God, come in human form to be man's Saviour.

In Heaven there are "golden vials full of odours, which are the prayers of saints" (Rev. 5:8). So the sweet perfume of frankincense offered by these wise men pictures the prayer and praise that is due God. By their gifts, the wisemen acknowledged the deity of Christ, and worshiped Him as God.

Myrrh—the Bitter Spice Shows Faith in a Suffering Saviour

Gold and frankincense and myrrh the wise men gave to Jesus when they opened their treasures and gave Him gifts. As the gold pictures tribute to a king and the frankcense pictures prayer and praise to a God, so the myrrh presents, we believe, faith in Jesus as Saviour, suffering, dying, atoning for man's sin.

For myrrh was one of the bitter spices used for burying. We learn that when Joseph of Arimathea took down the body of Jesus from the cross, he and Nicodemus prepared the body for burial with myrrh and aloes. John 19:39 and 40 say:

"And there came also Nicodemus, which at the first came to Jesus by night, and brought a mixture of myrrh and aloes, about an hundred pound weight. Then took they body of Jesus, and wound it in linen clothes with the spices, as the manner of the Jews is to bury."

Surely myrrh means mourning and anointing for the dead. The myrrh and aloes are a picture of suffering. And these wise men were taught by the Holy Spirit that Jesus would die for sinners, and they came trusting Him as Saviour.

The Lord told Moses out in the wilderness to prepare holy anointing oil, and the first of the elements in this ointment was myrrh. Exodust 30:22 to 25 tells us:

"Moreover the Lord spake unto Moses, saying, Take thou also unto thee principal spices, of pure myrrh five hundred shekels, and of sweet cinnamon half so much, even two hundred and fifty shekels, and of sweet calamus two and fifty shekels, And of cassia five hundred shekels, after the shekel of the sanctuary, and of oil olive an hin; And thou shalt make it an oil of holy ointment, an ointment compounded after the art of the apothecary; it shall be an holy anointing oil."

This holy anointing oil was used to anoint the tabernacle, the ark of the testimony, and other things that were pictures and types of the coming Saviour, pictures of atonement for sin by the shedding of blood. Myrrh was the first spice to be put into this ointment. So myrrh surely points to a Saviour who suffered and died for sinners.

Before the children of Israel came out of Egypt they were told to kill a passover lamb, one for each family. It was to be a male lamb, perfect and without blemish, picturing our dear, sinless Saviour. The blood of this passover lamb was to be put upon the door, and the death angel, seeing the blood upon the door, would pass by, and the firstborn would be spared. This passover lamb was to be roasted with fire and eaten with unleavened bread, and "with bitter herbs they shall eat it" (Exod. 12:8). As the passover lamb roasted with fire pictured Jesus undergoing the wrath of God for sin, so the bitter herbs picture also the sufferings of Christ for sinners. We do not know what these bitter herbs were but one of them may well have been myrrh.

It certainly seems that the myrrh pictured the sufferings of our Saviour, vicarious suffering, the innocent one atoning for the guilty.

We may well believe that all the long journey these wise men made from the East through the heat of the desert sun, with hearts torn between expectant hope and anxiety, each one searched his heart. Ah, they were sinners as all mankind are sinners. They could not have deceived themselves. As they went to seek God and His Saviour, the Baby Jesus, they must surely have been conscious of their guilt and sought for some way to forgiveness and peace of heart. Very likely already God had shown them that He loved sinners. Some way the Holy Spirit of God taught them that this King of the Jews whom they sought would also be a Saviour from sin. In fact, the only Scriptures they had in Daniel spoke of this Prince who should "finish transgressions and make an end of sins" (Dan. 9:24). So they somehow realized that the One whom they sought would be not only a King, not only God, but Saviour from sin. With trembling faith of children, these men with wise hearts, (hearts made wise by the teaching of the Holy Spirit Himself), they trusted themselves, sinners all, to the hands of the Saviour they sought. And so when they found Him they opened their treasures and took out the myrrh which pictured His sufferings, His atoning death, His sacrifice for sinners!

Oh, that men today were as wise as these wise men from the East! It would be all in vain to come and bring your gold to the Lord Jesus Christ and call Him King, if there were not a way to have sins forgiven. It would be all in vain to admit that He was God, the Creator, the Giver of every good and perfect gift, the God who hears prayer, if one could not see that He also is the forgiver of sins, God's atoning sacrifice to make peace with mankind. The Lord Jesus is surely King and deserves our tribute. He is certainly the mighty God and deserves all the praise of our lips and all the frankincense of prayer. But much more, praise God, He is the "one mediator between God and men" (I Tim. 2:5). He is the Lamb of God that takes away the sin of the world. He is our Passover sacrificed for us. We are redeemed, not with corruptible things as silver and gold, but with the precious blood of Christ.

Concerning the birth of our Lord Jesus Christ, this idea of Him as a Saviour was ever the most prominent one. The angel said to Joseph before His birth, "Thou shalt call his name JESUS: *for he shall save his people from their sins*" (Matt. 1:21). His precious name, Jesus, means Saviour! To the shepherds in the field feeding their flocks by night, the angel of God that great night gave the glad tidings, "For unto you is born this day a SAVIOUR which is Christ the Lord." It would be no good news just that a king was born, for kings have been born before and none ever saved a man from sin. Even if the angel should announce that God had come down to visit men, that would not necessarily mean peace. God came down at Mount Sinai, the mountain burned with fire, the people trembled and Moses himself said, "I exceedingly fear and quake." The ministration of the law was glorious, but it was a glory that led to death and condemnation, and when God spoke to the people it was "thou shalt not" all the way through the Ten Commandments.

No, the baby born that day was to be King and worthy of the gifts of gold, and was to be Deity and worthy of the frankincense representing praise and prayer, but if He were not to be really an atoning Saviour, then all of God's plan is gone awry, and mankind is left in darkness and shadow of death! Thank God, when the wise men had given their gold and given their frankincense, they could also bring myrrh, by faith in the suffering, atoning, dying Saviour who paid once for all for man's sins and tore away the veil in the temple so that man could approach God in peace!

How well old Simeon knew this as he waited in the temple until the Baby Jesus was presented and then held Him in his arms! And then he could say by faith, turning to Mary, "Yea, a sword shall pierce through thy own soul also" (Luke 2:35). He had in mind the crucifixion. And God had in mind the crucifixion! And the angels had in mind the crucifixion! So these wise men from the East had in mind the crucifixion, a cross, an atonement, a sacrifice for sin, when they opened their treasures and brought out myrrh!

When Mary of Bethany anointed the Saviour with sweet-smelling spices and ointment of spikenard, He said, "Let her alone: against the day of my burying hath she kept this" (John 12:7).

It is my humble prayer that every reader of these lines may, with humble and contrite heart, look up by faith to-day to Jesus Christ and bring out the myrrh, that is, the faith of your sin-weary heart, and trust Jesus Christ as Saviour. Pay Him tribute as King; yes, worship Him as God of very God, yes, oh yes! He deserves it all! But above everything else, dear reader, I beg you trust Him as your own Saviour dying for sin and paying all that sinners were ever due to give to God. Trust Him today to be your sacrifice and make your peace with the Father. Give Him the gold, yes, and the frankincense and above everything else, bring Him the myrrh, the faith in His dying and loving atonement for sin.

Be Wise, Bring Jesus Your Gifts.

It is my earnest prayer that every reader of these lines will open his treasures and bring to the Lord Jesus Christ all the best and sweetest of the things dear to Him. Will you bring the Lord Jesus your gold? Will you offer to Him your full allegiance and take Him as Lord? The tithes and offerings that you bring ought simply to mean a surrendered heart. It ought to mean that God owns the title to all you possess and has a right to your full allegiance. I hope you will give it today. How sweet it would be if many who read this would say, "Today, God being my helper, I will put Jesus Christ first and crown Him Lord of all in my life." Thus will you enter into the sweet surrender and worship of the wise men who brought their gold to Jesus.

And out of the deep treasures of your heart will you give Lord Jesus His due as God? Will you offer Him all praises of your heart? Will you name His blessings, will you acknowledge your indebtedness, will you thank Him as Creator and Upholder of all things, the One from whose bountiful hand every blessing flows? This is what the wise men meant when they offered Him the frankincense of praise and prayer. Why not make it the settled policy of your life that your heart will overflow with praise? Whether thanks at the table or a grateful prayer on rising, or public testimony when opportunity affords, or the simple, never-ceasing adoration of a grateful heart—oh, I beg you, give Jesus Christ, our Lord, His due as deity, as God, a good God, a bountiful God, a loving God. Come to Him with your burdens; offer Him your prayers. Call upon Him in the day of trouble. Ask whatsoever you will of the Father in His name that your joy may be full. Let the sweet incense, the odors which are the prayers of the saints, glorify Jesus Christ as God.

And if you have never bowed your heart in simple faith to Jesus as your own Saviour, will you do it today? As wise men, with trembling and eager fingers, sought out the precious scented packages of myrrh from their bundles, they must have had tears for the sufferings that Jesus would bear for them. They must have had some intangible sense of His death on the cross for all mankind. We do not know what swelling of love and surrender and faith were in their hearts. We simply know that they meant to express their faith in Him as the Lamb of God who would die for man's sin. They loved Him, they worshiped Him and they trusted Him as Saviour. Will you do the same today?

Many of you have longed to be Christians. You have, thought that one day you would be. Then will you not today with a wise heart, a heart wise with the wisdom of God, a heart led by the same Holy Spirit who prompted these wise men as they brought their treasures—out of such a heart will you trust Jesus Christ as your Saviour today? If you will do so—and how I hope you will—won't you please write and let us rejoice together in this wonderful Saviour?

And these wise men went "back another way". I trust that you will live a different life from the very moment that you, with swelling, glad heart of faith, bow to Jesus as Lord and King, and worship Him as God and trust Him as Saviour.

A Christmas Decision for Sinners

Here is a decision slip to help you to decide and to help express your decision, if today you will bring the Lord Jesus Christ all the treasures of your heart, as did these wise men.

Date _____

Shelton L. Smith
Murfreesboro, TN
Dear Dr. Smith:

As the sweet associations of the Christmas season come, I want, like the wise men of old, to bring to Jesus Christ the best gifts out of my treasures. Depending on God for help, I sincerely and earnestly covenant that:

(1) I will claim Christ as my Lord and King and offer Him full possession of everything that I have as pictured by the gold of the wise men. All earthly possessions I will try to use for His glory or give where He leads.

(2) I do gladly acknowledge His deity, that Jesus is the Son of God and I will earnestly try to honor Him by praise for all of His blessings and prayer for all my needs, knowing that God gives my blessings and God is willing to my prayers if I come in Jesus' name.

(3) I believe that Jesus Christ died for my sins and so as the wise men brought Jesus myrrh to symbolize His death and faith in the atonement that Jesus made, I here and now trust Jesus Christ as my Saviour, depend upon

Him to forgive all my sins. Today I claim Him as my Saviour as well as my Lord and my God. I write this as an open confession that I depend on Jesus Christ as my own personal Saviour today.

Signed _____

Address _____

No Room for Jesus!

"And she brought forth her firstborn son, and wrapped him in swaddling clothes, and laid him in a manger; because there was no room for them in the inn".—Luke 2:7.

POOR MARY! I can imagine that she was only a girl of eighteen or nineteen when the Baby Jesus was born; Jewish girls married young. And did ever a woman come to the hour of travail in more distressing circumstances? She was away from home. Caesar Augustus at Rome had decreed that "all the world should be taxed... and all went to be taxed, every one into his own city." So Joseph and Mary came from the province of Galilee, out of their little city, Nazareth, to Bethlehem. They were both descended from King David and proud of that they were. So they must come to the city of David to register, and I suppose they paid a small poll tax. How strange it was that they must come just at this time when Mary was great with child. Did they understand why?

God was fulfilling His Word. In Micah 5:2 it was written, "But thou, Bethlehem Ephratah, though thou be little among the thousands of Judah, yet out of thee shall he come forth unto me that is to be ruler in Israel; whose goings forth have been from of old, from everlasting." So

Caesar Augustus, not knowing why, gave the decree that all the world should be taxed, and the millions of the Roman Empire must go and register, unconscious that thereby God was bringing Mary and Joseph to Bethlehem the Saviour might be born there and so one verse of Scripture be fulfilled!

Women sometimes have strange fears and forebodings before the birth of a child. It is part of the curse which fell on womankind when the guilty pair were put outside the Garden of Eden. And this was to be Mary's firstborn! Her mother was not at hand nor any of the godly, elderly women of the community who would always know just what to do in such a case. There was no physician, nor a midwife even. Oh, if only Cousin Elisabeth could be here who had only six months before borne a child and named him John! She and Elisabeth were very dear to each other and had blessed, high hopes in common.

No, with her was only poor Joseph. Joseph was only a man and as helpless as she. Men seem ignorant and clumsy enough at best in such matters. Joseph was so kind and tender. With a holy restraint, he had cared for his virgin wife. But he was not in fact a husband as yet. How desperately alone Mary must have felt when at first she feared, and then she knew, that her baby was to be born here in Bethlehem among strangers and far away from her little Nazareth home! It would have been bad enough, she doubtless thought, if they could have had a nice, clean, quiet room in a private home or even the courtesy of a common tavern or a hotel. But the town was full. David had many other descendants who had come, likewise, to register. There was no room for them in the inn. In Mary's hour of travail when she slipped down into the valley of shadows, her bed was nothing but straw in a stable. And when her baby was born, she herself, with trembling yet glad fingers, wrapped her Babe in swaddling clothes and laid Him in a manger "because there was no room for them in the inn!"

Poor Joseph

And poor Joseph, too! God be praised for the memory of faithful, believing, godly Joseph. For one thing he loved Mary tenderly. Can you imagine his broken heart when he first had been compelled to believe that she had gone wrong, had been untrue to him and was to have an illegitimate child? But Joseph had not acted hastily. With earnest thought and prayer he sought to find what to do and was "minded to put her away privily" because he was a just man and not willing to see Mary stoned as an adulteress. "But while he thought on these things, behold, the angel of the Lord appeared unto him in a dream, saying, Joseph, thou son of David, fear not to take unto thee Mary thy wife: for that which is conceived in her is of the Holy Ghost. And she shall bring forth a son, and thou shalt call is name JESUS: for he shall save his people from their sins (Matt. 1:20,21).

The angel told him that this was to be the fulfillment of Isaiah 7:14, that a virgin should conceive and bring forth a Son and they should call His name Immanuel or God with us: God in human form. Joseph believed it and "being raised from sleep did as the angel of the Lord had bidden him, and took unto him his wife: And knew her not till she had brought forth her firstborn son: and he called his name JESUS" (Matt. 1:24,25). Not fearing the shame of clacking tongues, Joseph took Mary to his home, not doubting a moment the promise of God through the angel. With confident high hopes he rejoiced with Mary that she had found favor with God and was to be the mother the Saviour, the promised Messiah. With a manly restraint, he took Mary to his home and yet "knew her not till she had brought forth her firstborn son."

Can you imagine the concern of Joseph as they plodded from house to house in Bethlehem? We suppose that he led the donkey on which Mary rode. But every door was closed. There was no room. If Joseph had a little money from his carpenter shop, he did not have enough. The competion was too keen. Others with better standing or more money or first claim were given the rooms, and Joseph and Mary had none. At last they went to the little inn, the only one in the village of Bethlehem, I suppose, and there again they found there was no room. Joseph must have felt a little of the shame which every good man of breeding feels when he finds himself unable to provide for his family as they need and deserve. He must have expressed his sorrow to Mary many a time, and she, sustained by an unfaltering faith and surrounded surely by unseen heavenly beings, doubtless reassured Joseph many a time that God would provide. There was no room for them in the inn, and so they found poor refuge in a stable, and there the Saviour was born and laid in a manger.

It Was Jesus for Whom They Had No Room!

Alas, we well know that the world has no quarrel with Mary nor with Joseph. This world has a quarrel with Jesus Christ. Other babies were born in Bethlehem and their mothers had clean linen and soft beds and tender care. Other young heads of families were as poor as Joseph, and yet they had more friends and more comfort in the hour of trouble than Joseph had. There would have been room for Mary or room for Joseph. The simple truth is that there was no room for Jesus!

We are not to think that it was a meaningless incident that Christ was born in a stable and laid in a manger. God had the millions of the Roman world to register for taxation at a certain time so that one verse of Scripture should be fulfilled and His Son should be born in Bethlehem, then we may be sure that every detail surrounding this whole event is fraught with a weight of meaning. The time was fulfilled. From the beginning of the ages God had planned every detail of the coming of His dear Son into the world to save men. "When the fulness of the time was come, God sent forth his Son, made of a woman, made under the law, To redeem them that were under the law, that we might receive the adoption of sons." It is unthinkable that any detail of the birth of Christ could fail to have a universal meaning for the race. And so when there was no room for them in the inn, it was only a token of the fact that this world has no room for Jesus. It had no room then; it has none now. If any one ever doubted the wickedness of the race, the depravity to which mankind has fallen, let him but remember that there was no room for Jesus. I have often thought that the death of Christ on the cross revealed the awful wickedness of the human heart as nothing else could. The Holy Jesus was hated, despised, betrayed, denied, scourged, spit upon, crowned with thorns, given vinegar and gall, nailed to the cross, mocked while He died between thieves, and then pierced with the spear! What sinners we are! Christ rejected by priests and scribes, hated by Pharisees, suspicioned by Pilate, jeered by the multitude, crucified by all! What a revelation of the heart of mankind! But if all that was revealed in the death of Christ, just as surely it was symbolized when there was no room for the Saviour to be born in a decent house in Bethlehem, and He was born in a stable and laid in a manger! No room for Jesus!

The incident occurred, not because each home in Bethlehem, and the innkeeper, too, conspired to shut out Jesus purposely. No, they did not know—but they did not know because they did not care! And God had it occur so, and recorded it here, we believe, to be a true picture of the world's attitude toward Christ.

When Did the Baby Jesus Know the World Did Not Want Him?

We cannot fathom all the mystery of divinity, incarnate God in human flesh. We do not know just how much of His infinite wisdom Christ left with the Father in Heaven along with His robes of glory. How soon did the Baby Jesus come to know all that went on about Him? In John 2:25 we are told that Jesus "needed not that any should testify of man: for he knew what was in man." But in Luke 2:52, when Jesus was a child, the Scripture says that "Jesus increased in wisdom and stature, and in favour with God and man."

When the baby eyes of Jesus opened first, they saw the dingy outlines of a stable. The first sensation of the tender skin of the Baby may have been of the rough, torn cloth of His swaddling band or the pricking of straw in the manger. And the Son of God heard through those little human ears the munching of hay by an ox or an ass, perhaps, in the same stable. The Saviour had emptied Himself of much of His glory and of some of the attributes of deity before coming to dwell in this tiny body formed in the womb of a virgin. None of us can know until we get to Heaven just how much the Child knew, just how soon He realized that He was the very Son of God, the Creator of the heavens and earth, the Saviour of the world. These matters belong in the holy treasury of knowledge where human feet have never trod. If angels know these mysteries they have never whispered them, and the Holy Spirit of God has never breathed them into the ears of His prophets to set them down. Yet it stabs at my heart with shame to feel that the Baby Jesus, as soon as He knew anything, must have known that He was an unwanted Child, sent to redeem a world that hated Him, born more for death than life. He was slain before the foundation of the world, both in the heart of God who gave Him, and in His own redeeming love who planned it with the Father; but equally slain throughout time in the foreknown wickedness and malice and godless indifference of a world that had no room for Jesus!

Whenever the Baby Jesus came to know that He was the coming King of the Jews, the Saviour of mankind, the very Son of God; whether that was from the first instant that He, the pre-existent Christ, entered into the quickened body or whether later Jesus came into the realization of His humanity, Jesus was certainly aware of a hostile and indifferent world. How soon did He hear from the lips of His mother of the death of those other babies of Bethlehem, slain by Herod in the hope of destroying the King of the Jews? How soon did He know of those scribes and chief priests who knew that the Saviour should be born in Bethlehem because it was foretold by the Prophet Micah and who knew that the time was at hand and had met the wise men in the East, and yet themselves would not go the six miles to Bethlehem to see the Saviour? Do you suppose He marveled that the courts at Rome and in provinces around the world went on undisturbed by His advent? Do you suppose He thought it strange that a few poor shepherds from the field and some Magi from the East were all who visited the Saviour of mankind, the Son of God, the Creator of the worlds and the coming King?

Jesus Knew Men Would Hate Him But, Loving, He Came.

Do not misunderstand. When Jesus first learned of the wicked indifference and the active hate of this world, it was no surprise. He knew the malice of sinful men before He gave Himself to live and die for them. Before the Son came to these wicked husbandmen, already He had sent many servants, the prophets (Matt. 21:33-46). It was revealed long ago in the Old Testament that He was to be despised and rejected, a Man of sorrows and acquainted with grief (Isa. 53:3). He was to be before the people as a Root out of dry ground without form or comeliness (Isa. 3:2). When they saw Him, they would see no beauty that they should desire Him. He who through the Holy Spirit inspired the account of the crucifixion in Psalm 22, He who had pictured it to the Jews through the roasted passover lamb and millions of dying sacrifices, knew what to expect of mankind. It was already foretold that His face would be more marred than any man (Isa. 52:14). Long ago He had had the prophet inscribe about Him that He would set His face like a flint (Isa. 50:7) toward the sufferings of the cross. I say that Jesus knew ahead of time there would be no room for Him in the inn, no room at all in the hearts of most of the people of this world and in their business and governments and schools and homes and lives. He was to be gladly received by the few: the shepherds, the wise men, Anna, Simeon, Zacharias and Elizabeth, Mary and Joseph, with some publicans and harlots and occasional others. He was to arouse a passing interest in the multitudes when He fed the five thousand or preached the sermon on the mount or healed the sick or raised the dead, but that was soon to pass into growing indifference, then irritation and animosity, and multitudes would grow to hate Him with an unceasing and satanic hate when the venom of sin would do its worst to the Son of God in human form.

The story of the life of Christ on earth is summed up in this brief verse of Luke 2:7, "And she brought forth her firstborn son, and wrapped him in swaddling clothes, and laid him in a manger; because there was NO ROOM FOR THEM IN THE INN."

No Room Anywhere Among Men!

There was no room for the Baby Jesus in the inn at Bethlehem.

There was no room for Him permanently anywhere else as He wandered up and down this earth for "the foxes have holes, and the birds of the air have nests; but the Son of man hath not where to lay his head" (Matt 8:20). "When every man went unto his own house, Jesus went unto the mount of Olives" (John 7:53 and 8:1). Doubtless He slept alone in the mount more than once, and He and His disciples ate the wheat by the roadside. And even that was begrudged them because it was the Sabbath (Matt. 12:1,2).

There was no room for the anointed Son of God in His own synagogue and village of Nazareth. They hated Him and would have killed Him (Luke 4:29).

There was no room for Him even in His mother's and brothers' home "for neither did his brethren believe in him" (John 7:5). His brothers and even His mother sought to stay Him from His preaching (Mark 3:31–35). Even His friends thought Him mad for what He did (Mark 3:21).

There was no room for Him in Gadara and "they be-sought him that he would depart out of their coasts"—
(Matt. 8:34).

There was no room for Him in Jerusalem for they took up stones to cast at Him (John 8:59).

Yea, there was no room for Him in the whole world, and so Herod and Pontius Pilate and the chief priests and scribes, the Pharisees and Sadducees, the mob of common people and Roman soldiers all agree together that He must die. NO ROOM FOR JESUS!

Wicked Men Begrudged Jesus All He Ever Had.

In Bethlehem they begrudged the Son of God even a place to be born for there was no room for them in the inn.

Herod begrudged Him His kingly title and sought to slay him. The people of Nazareth begrudged Him His fame and said, "Is not "this the carpenter's son? is not his mother called Mary? and his brethren, James, and Joses, and Simon, and Judas? And his sisters, are they not all with us? Whence then hath this man all these things? And they were offended in him" (Matt. 13:55–57).

The Pharisees begrudged Him His power and said, "This fellow doth not cast out devils, but by Beelzebub the prince of the devils" (Mat. 12:24).

They begrudged His right in His own Father's house and said, "By what authority doest thou these things? and who gave thee this authority?" (Matt. 21:23) when He cleansed the temple of worldlings and thieves.

The chief priests begrudged Him the Sabbath of which He was Lord because He therein healed the sick and made whole the withered hand (Matt. 12:10).

They begrudged Him even the homage of harlots and publicans and murmured "This man receiveth sinners, and eateth with them" (Luke 15:2).

They begrudged Him every feast that was given, saying, "Behold, a man gluttonous, and a winebibber" (Matt 11:19).

And Simon the Pharisee begrudged Him even the tears and kisses upon His feet, dried with the hair of a forgiven streetwalker, the woman who was a sinner, and swore therefore that He was not a prophet (Luke 7:36-50).

Judas Iscariot begrudged Him the sweet perfume of the alabaster box of ointment broken for Him by the love of Mary (John 12:3-8).

The chief priests begrudged Him even the cries of little children, Hosanna in the highest, though the very rocks would have cried out had they been hushed (Mark 11:9; Luke 19:37-40).

They begrudged Him even an hour of prayer when He sweat drops of blood in the Garden of Gethsemane and broke into it with their torches, swords and staves, to kiss Him with a traitor's kiss, to bind Him and lead Him away to trial and murder (Matt. 26:47—68).

Even in His death the senseless malice of a wicked race of men had no room for Jesus.

The rulers begrudged His name, "The King of the Jews," nailed above His cross and begged Pilate to change it (John 19:21).

They begrudged Him even His clothes in the hour of His shame and stripped Him, naked, seamless garment and all (Ps. 22:18; John 19:23,24).

They begrudged Him even a drink of water when in

His dying agony He said, I thirst. Instead of water they gave Him vinegar and gall (John 19:28,29; Matt. 27:34).

They begrudged His poor, tired body even the peace that death brought, so after He had given up the ghost, they pierced a spear deep into His side, and there came out water and blood.

They begrudged even the testimony that His hanging body gave to the world, of their sin and His love. They hastened to take the body down before sunset. They had room for Jesus even then.

And when He rose from the dead they begrudged Him even this proof that He was the Son of God. They gave large sums of money unto the soldiers, "Saying, Say ye, His disciples came by night, and stole him away while we slept. And if this come to the governor's ears, we will persuade him, secure you. So they took the money, and did as they were taught: and this saying is commonly reported among Jews until this day" (Matt. 28:12-15).

And today men begrudge Him His miracles, begrudge His virgin birth, His bodily resurrection, even the inspiration of His words. They begrudge Him His deity, His hold on the hearts of men. The race hates Him for His claims as the only Saviour of mankind!

GREAT GOD OF MERCY, REMEMBER NOT OUR INIQUITIES AGAINST US! This undone, corrupted, iniquitous world of mankind has no room for Jesus!

Reader, have you no room for Jesus? Have you crowded Him out of your heart? Have you no time to serve Him, no time for His Word, no time to pray?

Poor, lost sinner, is not your heart convicted of your terrible sin in crowding Christ out? Will you go to Hell because you have no room in your heart for the Son of God?

Will you spend eternity in torment because pleasure or self-will or sin in any form bars the door of your heart against Jesus? Oh! Let Him in! Let Him in today! Christ brings sweet peace. You can never have peace without Him. He brings salvation, but "there is none other name under heaven given among men, whereby we must be saved." Christ gives everlasting life, but He that believeth not is condemned already.

Most of the world has no room for Jesus. But those few that received Him, how happy they were and how blessed!

> *"He came unto his own, and his own received him not. But as many as received him, to them gave he power to become the sons of God, even to them that believe on his name."*—John 1:11,12.

Receive Him today! By faith take Him as yours. Open your heart and with tender love take Jesus in. You will never have a real Christmas without Him. But if you have Him you can laugh at poverty, you can rejoice in adversity, you can look death in the face unafraid. If you have Jesus, you have all that God can give a poor, rebellious race! Take Him today.

No Room in the Inn

No beautiful chamber,
No soft cradle bed,
No place but a manger,
Nowhere for His head;

No praises of gladness,
No thought of their sin,
No glory but sadness,
No room in the inn.

No sweet consecration,
No seeking His part,

No humiliation,
No place in the heart:

No thought of the Saviour,
No sorrow for sin,
No prayer for His favor,
No room in the inn.

No one to receive Him,
No welcome while here,
No balm to relieve Him,
No staff but a spear;

No seeking His treasure,
No weeping for sin,
No doing His pleasure,
No room in the inn.

Chorus

No room, no room for Jesus
Oh, give Him welcome free,
Lest you should hear at Heaven's gate,
There is no room for thee.

Make a Decision Today to Include Jesus

If you will today make room for Jesus in your heart, take Him as your Saviour, trust Him to forgive you, claim Him now openly once and for all as your Lord and your Saviour, then write me today. Can you honestly sign this, copy it, and send it?

Date: _____

Shelton L. Smith
Murfreesboro, TN
Dear Dr. Smith:

I am ashamed that I did not have room for Jesus before today. Here and now I open my heart and trust Him for forgiveness and receive Him as my Saviour. I believe that He forgives me now. I ask Him to save my soul and keep me because He died for me and loves me and because I trust Him.

Name _____

Address _____

Immanuel—God With Us

"Therefore the Lord himself shall give you a sign; Behold, a virgin shall conceive, and bear a son, and shall call his name Immanuel."—Isa. 7:14.

HERE IS a Christmas Scripture, a verse in the Old Testament that speaks about the birth of the Baby Jesus, God's own Son, who was born of a virgin mother, lived among men, died for our sins on the cross, and arose again and ascended into Heaven. The Prophet Isaiah, nearly 750 years before the Saviour was born, wrote by divine inspiration, "Therefore the Lord himself shall give you a sign; Behold, a virgin shall conceive, and bear a son, and shall call his name Immanuel."

This verse was later quoted by the angel of God, speaking to Joseph, the promised husband of Mary. The record is given us in Matthew 1:23. So we know that this verse, written by the prophet of God long beforetime, tells of the birth of Jesus Christ.

The virgin birth is a sign, we are told. The preceding verse says that it is a sign given to the house of David. Of course it was not addressed simply to Ahaz, but to the whole house of David. So Mary, who was of the lineage

77

of David, and Joseph, her promised husband, who was also descended from Israel's greatest king, were doubtless familiar with this Old Testament verse. And so each of them found it easy to believe the prophecy of God that the dear Lord Jesus was to be born without a human father, born a virgin mother.

The New Testament quotation of this verse gives the interpretation of the word *Immanuel*. Matthew 1:23 tells us, "Behold, a virgin shall be with child, and shall bring forth a son, and they shall call his name Emmanuel, which being interpreted is, God with us." *Immanuel* (spelled Emmanuel in the New Testament) means God with us. What a wonderful thought for Christmas! The dear Lord Jesus is called "God with us."

1. The Virgin Birth Essential to Christ's Deity

How like the characteristic straightforward way of the Bible, to tell us first that a virgin should conceive and bear a son and then tell us that this virgin-born Son, without a human father, should be called Immanuel, "God with us." Here the Bible simply expresses an obvious fact: the deity of Christ depends upon His virgin birth. Jesus Christ was not born as other people are: He is not the son of a human father. Rather, He was miraculously conceived in the womb of a virgin. The Spirit of God Himself miraculously caused the conception of the Lord Jesus.

All who understand the simplest, plainest doctrines in the Bible will understand why the Saviour must be born of a virgin. Men are tainted with sin. The whole race is fallen since Adam and Eve sinned in the Garden of Eden. Every child ever born comes into this world with the curse of sin upon him. Every child is born but to die. And if Jesus were to be without the taint of sin, He needed to be conceived and born in a way different from the usual course of mankind. He was conceived and born of a virgin. Jesus had no human father!

Wicked men who did not want to honor Jesus as the Christ of God, who were not willing to bow to Him as their Lord and Saviour, have falsely stated that the Hebrew word for *virgin,* in Isaiah 7:14, did not necessarily mean *virgin,* but only a young woman, whether married or single. But that statement is as unscholarly as it is malicious. The word here used for *virgin,* the Hebrew word *almah,* is used six other times in the Old Testament. I have just read the six other verses in the Bible which use this word, and even a casual reader would be convinced that the meaning is as translated in Isaiah 7:14, a virgin. One case is that of Miriam, the sister who watched the baby Moses in the bulrushes and went and called his mother for the princess who found him. Another is of Rebekah before she was married, and the term is used in his prayer by the godly servant who came to find a bride for Isaac. In one such verse, Song of Solomon 6:8, the word is used to differentiate certain serving girls from the concubines and queens of Solomon! The virgins were not concubines, were not queens; that is, they were not married, and they were literally virgins. The other times also the word is well translated simply virgin, or maid, as distinguished from married woman or matron.

But there is an easier way for us to understand the meaning of the term virgin as used here in Isaiah 7:14, and that is to see how the New Testament explains it. Joseph was deeply concerned when he found that Mary, to whom he was engaged, would soon have a child. Had Mary played the harlot? Had she, whom he had so loved and trusted, gone into sin, and was she about to become an unwed mother as the result of her sin? How he loved Mary! Must he renounce her and accuse her before the authorities and have her stoned to death as an adulteress? While these things troubled the poor heart of Joseph, he fell asleep, and the angel of God appeared to him. The story is given in Matthew 1:18–25. Let us read it with reverence and joy:

> "Now the birth of Jesus Christ was on this wise: When as his mother Mary was espoused to Joseph, before they came together, she was found with child of the Holy Ghost. Then Joseph her husband, being a just man, and not willing to make her a publick example, was minded to put her away privily. But while he thought on these things, behold, the angel of the Lord appeared unto him in a dream, saying, Joseph, thou son of David, fear not to take thee Mary thy wife: for that which is concieved in her is of the Holy Ghost. And she shall bring forth a son, and thou shalt call his name JESUS: for he shall save his people from their sins. Now all this was done, that it might be fulfilled which was spoken of the Lord by the prophet, saying, Behold, a virgin shall be with child, and shall bring forth a son, and they shall call his name Emmanuel, which being interpreted is God with us. Then Joseph being raised from sleep did as the angel of the Lord had bidden Him, and took unto him his wife: And knew her not till she had brought forth her firstborn son: and he called his name JESUS."

Here again we have the plain, simple statement that "that which is conceived in her [Mary] is of the Holy Ghost." And then we are told that this is simply a fulfillment of the promise in Isaiah 7:14 that a virgin should conceive and bear the Saviour, without a human father.

You see that the deity of Christ hangs upon His virgin birth.

And again in Luke the same question of the virgin

birth of Christ comes up. The Angel Gabriel came to Mary and gave her the wonderful promise that she should be the mother of the Saviour. Luke 1:26–38 tells the story:

> *"And in the sixth month the angel Gabriel was sent from God unto a city of Galilee, named Nazareth, to a virgin espoused to a man whose name was Joseph, of the house of David; and the virgin's name was Mary. And the angel came in unto her, and said, Hail, thou that art highly favoured, the Lord is with thee: blessed art thou among women. And when she saw him, she was troubled at his saying, and cast in her mind what manner of salutation this should be. And the angel said unto her, Fear not, Mary: for thou hast found favour with God. And, behold, thou shalt conceive in thy womb, and bring forth a son, and shalt call his name JESUS. He shall be great, and shall be called the Son of the Highest: and the Lord God shall give unto him the throne of his father David: And he shall reign over the house of Jacob for ever; and of his kingdom there shall be no end. Then said Mary unto the angel, How shall this be, seeing I know not a man? And the angel answered and said unto her, The Holy Ghost shall come upon thee, and the power of the Highest shall overshadow thee: therefore also that holy thing which shall be born of thee shall be called the Son of God. And, behold, thy cousin Elisabeth, she hath also conceived a son in her old age: and this is the sixth month with her, who was called barren. For with God nothing shall be impossible. And Mary said, Behold the handmaid of the Lord; be it unto me according to thy word. And the angel departed from her."*

Mary very properly asked the angel, "How shall this be, seeing I know not a man?"

The angel answered, "The Holy Ghost shall come upon thee, and the power of the Highest shall overshadow thee: therefore also that holy thing which shall be born of thee shall be called the Son of God."

This is the clear prophecy of a miracle. And the angel said, "For with God nothing shall be impossible." And it is only by virtue of this virgin birth, this miraculous conception, unlike the conception of every other child ever born, that Jesus is called in a unique sense, the Son of God. The deity of Christ depends upon His virgin birth.

Christmastime is a time to honor Christ, God's unspeakable Gift to men. Christmastime is a time to praise His name, to glorify Him, to give the dear Lord Jesus the honor which is His due. And no one can give Christ any proper honor who does not admit His virgin birth and, therefore, His deity.

Every believer in the Bible believes the virgin birth. One who does not believe in the virgin birth of Christ has no right to claim to be a Christian. Any so-called Christian leader or preacher or teacher who says that belief in the virgin birth is not essential is trifling with holy matters. Any such statement is a scandalous hypocrisy, an inexcusable evasion of the truth.

One who does not believe in the virgin birth of Christ should simply say, "I am not a Christian. I do not believe the Bible. I do not believe in the deity of Christ. I do not trust in His atoning blood. I am an infidel, a pagan." One who denies the virgin birth and pretends to be a Christian is a deliberate deceiver, using feigned words to accept a salary or to maintain a position of honor or to get some other gain by this false and wicked pretension of Christianity without a supernatural Christ. At Christmastime, it is well for us to remember that we wish all men well but accept no one as a Christian who does not take Jesus Christ for all He claims to be, the virgin-born Son of God.

In the December 4, 1948, *Saturday Evening Post*, Dr. E.

82

Stanley Jones is quoted as saying that he wants a united world church and that the only condition for membership would be the "mere affirmation...the recognition that Christ is the Son of God." Dr. Jones, the famous Methodist missionary and propagandist, simply mentions an affirmation which is already included in the avowed purpose of the National Council of Churches and the World Council of Churches. But the affirmation is not sincere on the part of many who join the National Council of Churches, and Dr. Jones will forgive us if we must say that we do not believe he is sincere in proposing that single affirmation that Jesus is the Son of God as the one requirement of denominations for joining this super church he proposed. For, in fact, Dr. Jones is already the most active member of the National Council of Churches which he would make into a super church, to take away the independence of other denominations and join these denominations with the infidels and unbelievers already assembled under the name of the National Council of Churches! And in that council, Dr. Jones is bosom-friend and fellow-speaker of that infidel in bishop's robes, Dr. Oxnam, who, in an infamous speech, once declared that the God of the Old Testament was a dirty bully. Dr. Jones, who receives the Methodist infidel so gladly, knows that Oxnam does not pretend to believe that Jesus is the unique Son of God, that He is God come in the flesh. Dr. Jones is also the coworker of Dr. Harry Emerson Fosdick, who wrote the sermon, "The Peril of Worshiping Jesus" (*The Hope of the World*, pages 96 ff). There, Fosdick says that it is wrong to worship Jesus, that Jesus is not divine in any sense except in which others are divine also. That infidel with beautiful language, that messenger of Satan who comes as an angel of light, has been the boon companion of Dr. Jones, who prattles of getting everybody together, who affirms that they believe Jesus is the Son of God! Henry Sloane Coffin, Bishop Francis John McConnell, with Fosdick and Oxnam and many other modernists, call Jesus "Son of God", tongue in cheek, while they deny His virgin birth and His deity!

If any reader is offended by these plain words, then I challenge you that at Christmastime, the honor ought to be given to Jesus Christ and not to compromising preachers, not to pulpit infidels. If the deity of Christ and His virgin birth which proves it are offensive to men, then let be men offended, and let Christ still have the honor that belongs to Him as God incarnate! We can have no supernatural Christ without a supernatural birth. We can have no miracle Saviour without a miraculous birth. We cannot have Immanuel, God with us, unless He be born as the unique Son of God would be born. Christmas is only pagan tradition if Christ be not virgin-born, God in human form.

As the lovely Christmas carol sings:

> Silent night! Holy night!
> All is calm, all is bright
> 'Round yon virgin mother and Child!
> Holy Infant, so tender and mild.

All of historic Christianity revolves around the virgin birth of Jesus, the Son of God, born and laid in a manger at Bethlehem, worshiped by angels and shepherds and wise men—the Jesus who in later years was crucified on a Roman cross and poured out His blood to pay for our sins. The virgin-born Saviour is Immanuel, God with us, our Saviour and our God.

II. Christ Is Literally God With Us.

"...and shall call his name Immanuel. (Emmanuel in

New Testament spelling.) Mary called Jesus Emmanuel. And in Matthew 1:23, the verse is quoted with its interpretation, "And they shall call his name Emmanuel, which being interpreted is, God with us."

Immanuel, God with us! What a wonderful descriptive name of the dear Lord Jesus! He is "God with us". I hope that blessed and comforting truth may become a solid foundation on which we may rest forever! I hope that every reader will stop and let the intimate sweetness of this blessed truth move your heart and become a permanent part of your thinking. Jesus is "God with us".

1. Jesus Is Really God.

My book, *Is Jesus God?*, which is an answer to infidels in the church and out, was recently advertised in the SWORD OF THE LORD, and there came a critical letter from a man who said, "Of course, Jesus is not God. Jesus is the Son of God! How silly to write a book, *Is Jesus God?*" But he was as ignorant as he was irascible. Jesus is God, and the Scripture clearly says exactly that.

Let us go back again to that Gospel in the Old Testament, the book of Isaiah. There in Isaiah 9:6 is another Christmas Scripture, a prophecy of the birth of Jesus Christ. That verse says, "For unto us a child is born, unto us a son is given: and the government shall be upon his shoulder: and his name shall be called Wonderful, Counsellor, The mighty God, The everlasting Father, The Prince of Peace."

Did you note that this Child who is born to us and this Son who is given to us is called "The mighty God"! Jesus is God!

In Hebrews 1:8 is this startling statement, "But unto the Son he saith, Thy throne, O God, is for ever and ever:

a sceptre of righteousness is the sceptre of thy kingdom." Here in Hebrews 1:8 is a quotation from Psalm 45:6. The Old Testament Scripture says, "Thy throne, O God, is for ever and ever". Then Hebrews 1:8 says that statement is addressed to Jesus Christ the Son! God the Father addressing Jesus the Son says, "Thy throne, O God, is for ever and ever". Yes, Jesus is literally God. So a beautiful name of Christ is Immanuel, literally meaning, God with us. Jesus is God.

Does that seem strange to you? Then turn to the Gospel of John. There, in John 1:1,2, we have the following statement about Jesus who is called the Word.

"In the beginning was the Word, and the Word was with God, and the Word was God. The same was in the beginning with God."

In verse 14 of the same chapter, the Scripture says, "And the Word was made flesh, and dwelt among us, (and we beheld his glory, the glory as of the only begotten of the Father,) full of grace and truth."

This Word who was with God and was God, then, was made flesh. Jesus is God, but He is God with us! He is Immanuel!

I do not wonder that Thomas, who had been doubting the resurrection of the Saviour, when convinced by the nailprints and the wound in the side of the Saviour there before him, cried out and said, "My Lord and my God." Jesus is Immanuel; He really is God with us.

And the Bible everywhere teaches that Jesus is God. You remember that a rich young ruler came to Jesus and called Him, "Good Master," which is similar to good professor, or good rabbi. That did not please Jesus, for He is more than a teacher. And so Jesus replied, "Why callest thou me good? there is none good but one, that is God." If Jesus is not God, then He is not good, for He certainly claimed to be God, and He is an imposter and a deceiver unless He is what He claimed to be, God in human form.

We can have no Immanuel unless Christ is really God, unless Christ really is one with the Father.

2. In Christ, God Is With the Whole Human Race!

Immanuel is "God with us". God with the whole human race. In II Corinthians 5:19, the Scripture says, "To wit, that God was in Christ, reconciling the world unto himself, not imputing their trespasses unto them; and hath committed unto us the word of reconciliation." There is a sense in which Christ is not only God with Christians, but He is God with mankind. There is a sense in which the whole world is reconciled to God. Let us say, rather, that a bridge has been made between God and men, a bridge for the whole race to cross upon, if they will. Let us say that all the sinners who reject Christ and go to Hell were loved of God and sought of God and bought by the sacrifice of Calvary the same as the rest of us who have trusted and received the Saviour.

When God gave His Son, then God identified Himself forever with the human race. Christ, God the Son, even now sits in Heaven beside the Father, on the Father's throne, in a human body! When Christ comes again the second time, men will see the wounds in His hands and in His feet. When Christ was born, then, there is a sense in which God became a man. And God the Father and God the Son are so closely related, so perfectly united in thought and plan and will and work, that God the Father gave Himself when He gave His Son. And God the Father was eternally tied up with the human race when He gave His Son to be born of a virgin and to become Immanuel, "God with us".

I sometimes tell my daughters that they must remember that when they marry a young man, they marry his father and mother and brothers and sisters, too. So when God the Father gave His Son to become a man, God joined Himself to the whole human race. Christ is Immanuel, "God with us".

It is beautiful to remember that God made the sun, moon and stars as lights for man on this earth, that God created all the animal kingdom and the vegetable kingdom as realms over which man should have dominion. Of all created beings, man is to God the most precious. But now that Christ is born of a virgin and God the Son has become a man, then the godhead is forever to be occupied with the saving of men and God reveals Himself in human terms. God the Father is Father as an accommodation of the term a child uses for his parent. Christ is our high priest, as adaptation of a human office and a human term. Christ is the head and husband of His church, which is His body, including all the saved. But those are adaptations of human terms. God has the whole human race on His hands, and when God gave His Son to become Immanuel, it meant that God would be forever occupied with saving the human race, and that His delight would be in those of mankind who would trust in His Son. And His eternal companions in the glorious future will be sinners saved by grace! Christ is Immanuel, God with the whole human race.

III. Christ Is God With Me!

But for a born-again child of God, Christ is more than

God with the human race. Christ is, for the Christian, literally God with me! I can say like Thomas, when his doubts were dissolved, "My Lord and my God". Jesus is not only God—He is my God. He is not only God with mankind, but He is God with me!

"Christ in you, the hope of glory," says Colossians 1:27. Every Christian has Christ within. That is salvation, to have Christ. And those who have Christ have God the Father, also. In I John 5:12, we are told, "He that hath the Son hath life; and he that hath not the Son of God hath not life." Man is not saved because he is a member of a church, nor because he has followed certain rites and ceremonies, nor because he has committed certain worthy deeds. No! One is a Christian, one has salvation if he has God with him, if Christ Himself is within.

On that awesome night when Jesus talked to the frightened, troubled disciples in the upper room a few hours before His Gethsemane betrayal and arrest and trial and crucifixion, Jesus said, "If a man love me, he will keep my words: and my Father will love him, and we will come unto him, and make our abode with him" (John 14:23). And again Jesus said, "Yet a little while, and the world seeth me no more; but ye see me: because I live, ye shall live also. At that day ye shall know that I am in my Father, and ye in me, and I in you" (John 14:19,20). You see, the blessed Holy Spirit moves into the body of a Christian, and so God the Father and God the Son are forever with him.

The Holy Spirit of God constantly abides in the body of every Christian (Rom. 8:9, I Cor. 6:19,20). So the Christian can really say that he has Immanuel; that is, that God Himself is with the Christian.

And every Christian has the blessed promise of Jesus,

"And, lo, I am with you alway, even unto the end of the world." And then beyond the end of this age, we have the promise of eternal joy in His presence! One who has Christ has the Immanuel, has God with him. Christ is really God with me.

O, weak, stumbling Christians, how foolish for us not to see that Christ with us can solve every problem! He is the Creator of the worlds. We are plainly told, "All things were made by him; and without him was not any thing made that was made" (John 1:3). In Hebrews 1:2, we are plainly told that it was by his Son, Jesus Christ, by whom also he made the worlds. How can we fear hunger when the Creator of all the fields of the earth, the One from whose providential and loving hand every living creature in the universe is fed, is with us as our beloved, literally God with us and God within! How can we fear circumstances when the God of all circumstances is the God of grace, and He is with us! How can we fear sorrow and trouble when the God of all comfort is with us! Oh, the riches of love in Christ Jesus! Oh, the wealth of every Christian who has Christ! At Christmastime, every one of us might well muse and meditate on the wonderful gift at God gave and say with the inspired apostle, "Thanks be unto God for his unspeakable gift" (II Cor. 9:15). We have Immanuel! We have God with us!

Joshua had God with him, and so he could command the sun to stand still in the heavens, and it was so. King Hezekiah had God with him, and he could spread out the blasphemous letter of Sennacherib on the altar of the Lord, and the next morning the angel of God had slain 185,000 enemies besieging the city! The three Hebrew children had one "like the Son of God" to make a fourth in the fiery furnace. They literally had God with them. Christ, Immanuel, made that furnace into a pleasant walk. There was not the smell of fire on their garments, and not a hair of their heads was singed.

If I have needs, God has all the angels at His command, and they are "ministering spirits, sent forth to minister for them who shall be heirs of salvation" (Heb. 1:14). If I have God with me, I have all the angels of Heaven to be my messengers on the wings of light or my protectors with flaming swords! Hallelujah, when I have Immanuel, I have everything!

The morning this was written in the presence of other workers here in the Sword of the Lord office, I somewhat timidly asked God if in two days we could have the necessary $9,000 for taking the 2 per cent discount on some large printing bills just now due. In the prayer, I told God that there was no probable source from which such an amount would be humanly expected so soon but that He was the God of the impossible as well as of the probable. Others joined me in the prayer. We wanted another evidence of God's power, and we wanted to save $180 of the Lord's money by getting the cash discount. Within an hour after the prayer, I had in my hands a letter offering $5,000 immediately to be invested at reasonable interest in just such a matter as we needed to care for. The other $4,000 is at hand. Thus the money, within two days, will be provided, some of it income through regular sources and $5,000 of it through this unusual and unexpected source. I have had, perhaps a thousand such answers to definite prayers. One who has God has the wealth of the universe! Christ is Immanuel, God with us. Praise His name! Hallelujah, what a Saviour!

IV. Yet Those Without Christ Are Without God and Without Hope.

In Ephesians 2:12 is a plaintive and sad word about all who do not know Christ as Saviour. Speaking to the saints at Ephesus, Paul reminded them of the time when they were unsaved, in these words, "That at that time ye were without Christ, being aliens from the commonwealth of Israel, and strangers from the covenants of promise, having no hope, and without God in the world."

Any poor man or woman who does not have Christ does not have God. He is in a sad state, being an alien from God's people, a stranger to God's promises, "having no hope, and without God in the world". It is only in Christ that anyone is near to God, for Christ, Immanuel, is "God with us."

Years ago, I pressed upon a girl her duty to take Christ as her Saviour. She was not ready. She told me how good and moral she was. She, read the Bible. She prayed every day. She was modest and moral and upright.

"But to whom can you pray?" I asked her. "If you will not take Christ as Saviour, how could you pray?"

"I pray to God the Father," she said, "not to Jesus".

I assured her sadly that God the Father would never hear the prayer of one who rejected His Son. One who is without Christ is also without God in the world. There is no redemption, no salvation, no hope for any poor sin in the world outside of Jesus Christ!

One who will not have Christ cannot have the Holy Spirit dwelling in his body. One who will not have Christ cannot have God the Father manifesting Himself. One who will not have Christ cannot have forgiveness of sins, cannot have a home in Heaven, cannot have peace of heart. Christ is Immanuel, God with us. One who will not have Christ cannot have God.

How sad to have a Christmas without Christ! A day ago I was in the Loop shopping district of Chicago, and the streets were decorated with giant deer aloft on the light poles and connected with streamers of lights. Lighted Christmas trees are already gleaming in front windows of many homes. There is a rush of buying presents, wrapping packages and mailing beautiful Christmas cards. What a sad shame, what a disappointing and empty celebration is Chrismastime without Christ.

Is your joy in the bright Christmas tree with its lights and toys? The Christmas tree will soon be dragged out of the house to be burned or hauled away with the garbage! The pretty wrapping paper will be torn from the packages. The carefully placed seals will be broken and discarded. Mechanical toys will break their springs, and inquisitive little girls will poke the eyes out of doll babies. The mirth of the Christmas feasting and visiting will soon be over. And, oh, how soon the loved ones will be scattered to the end of the world! Some will die, and we will never see them again. Others will forget us and leave us lonely and disillusioned. How empty is a Christmas without Christ!

Some of you have a Bible but do not have the God of the Bible. You have the Book but do not have the Author! I do not wonder that you do not read it very much. The Book is a sealed Book. The things of God are not revealed to you by the Holy Spirit. For we are told, "But the natural man receiveth not the things of the Spirit of God: for they are foolishness unto him: neither can he know them, because they are spiritually discerned" (I Cor. 2:14). If you do not have Christ, the blessed Book of God may be to you dull and dry. It is a closed Book. There was a time when there were not many Bibles and when men chained the Bible to the pulpit so it could not be stolen. Oh, the Bible is a sealed and chained and locked Book to all whose empty hearts have not received the Author of the Book. If you do not have Immanuel, then you do not understand the Bible, and you do not have a teacher when you read it. Those who have a Christmas without a Christ, have a Bible without the Author.

In fact, if you do not have Christ, you have a world without a Creator. You do not know the riddle of the universe. It may be that your eyes are so blinded you do not even realize that God created this world and all that is in it. You cannot realize that He still administers this universe, still sustains it and that in Christ all things are held gether. If you do not have Christ, you do not realize that not a sparrow falls without His consent, that He clothes the lilies of the field, that all the hairs of your head are numbered. If you do not have Christ, then you cannot claim the promise that "all things work together for good them that love God, to them who are the called according his purpose." You have a world without the Creator. You have matter without the Mind behind it. Oh, if you not have Christ, you do not have God!

And, dear friend, if you do not have Christ, then you have sin and no remedy, sin and no Saviour!

I can well understand how, to the unconverted, Christmastime is a day of feasting and of drinking, a time of revelry and ribaldry. You cannot have the real sweetness of Christmas carols, for Christ is the center of them. You give your gifts, but you yourself, poor empty soul, cannot receive the things that satisfy! What do you know about Christmas joy anyway? You never heard the angel of

94

God say, "Fear not: for, behold, I bring you good tidings of great joy, which shall be to all people. For unto you is born this day in the city of David a Saviour, which is Christ the Lord!" Oh, wherever you are, whoever you are, you have your sin—but do you have a Saviour? Do you have cleansing for a black heart? Do you have peace for a troubled mind? Do you have a hope of eternal salvation, or do you have the fear of retribution, the certainty of punishment when your sins find you out? For all you who are sinners without a Saviour, let me say that the only remedy is to have Christ, Immanuel, God with us. For when He was born, the angel commanded, "And thou shalt call his name JESUS: for he shall save his people from their sins."

When Jesus was born in Bethlehem, Mary made her bed on the straw in a stable, and the Baby Jesus was wrapped in swaddling clothes and laid in a manger, "because there was no room for them in the inn." Someone reads this today who has made no room for Jesus. And do you know why you have rejected Christ? When you rejected Christ, you rejected God. And I fear, oh, I fear that was what you intended to do. You see, when Jesus was crucified, that was the first chance the world had ever had really to show how it felt about God. Never before did men have a chance to spit in the face of God! Never before did men have a chance to drive nails in His hands and feet, to pluck out His beard, to blindfold Him and smite Him and say, "Prophesy, who is it that smote thee?" Never before did people have a chance to look on while God died as the gentle victim of murderous men! Ever since the slaying of the animals whose skins were used to make coverings for Adam and Eve, down through the line of sacrifices, down through the death of good men and the martyrdom of saints, this old earth had soaked up much blood; but never until the dear Lord

95

Jesus died and there flowed out from the hole in His side, water mingled with blood, did this earth so cursed by sinful men ever soak up the blood of God!

You may be sure that men hated Jesus because He was God, not because He was man. You may be sure they hated Him because He was good, not because He was bad. You may be sure that men rejected Him because they did not want Him for what He is and what He was, God come in the flesh. He is Immanuel, "God with us"; and this God with us is the one they deliberately hated, rejected, and killed. Oh, sinner, hear me today! Do you reject Christ because He is the Christ of God? Do you reject Him because you do not want God?

This Christmastime is the best time you will ever have to receive Christ into your heart, to let Immanuel be your own Saviour, God with you! Why not today repent of your sins? Why not today turn to the Christ, the Saviour, and ask Him to come into your heart and forgive your sins and save your poor soul? Why not trust Him this moment, right now, to be your own Saviour now and forever? And the very moment that you turn your case over to Him, depend upon Him, risk Him, believe in Him, that moment He will be your own Immanuel, God with you, your Saviour, your constant companion, your eternal refuge from sin, your High Priest before God, your salvation!

If you will take this Christ as your own Saviour, then do it now, this day, this very hour! Let this be one Christmastime that you will have the Christ of Christmas; that you will have not only the Bible, but the one who wrote it; that you will have not only some of the good things of the world, but the one who made the world! Oh, let this be one Christmastime that you will have peace and forgiveness and salvation and redemption and a home in Heaven and a new heart! If you will take Christ as your Saviour, then here and now, this moment, close your eyes and honestly tell God so. Admit to Him that you are a sinner, earnestly ask Him to forgive you, and depend upon Him to do it this moment. Christ paid for your sins on the cross. He loves you. He is ready to receive you. And He has promised, "Him that cometh to me I will in no wise cast out." Then trust Him today!

The Virgin-Born Savior

"Therefore the Lord himself shall give you a sign; Behold, a virgin shall conceive, and bear a son, and shall call his name Immanuel."—Isa. 7:14.

"Now the birth of Jesus Christ was on this wise: When as his mother Mary was espoused to Joseph, before they came together, she was found with child of the Holy Ghost."—Matt. 1:18.

"Then said Mary unto the angel, How shall this be, seeing I know not a man? And the angel answered and said unto her, The Holy Ghost shall come upon thee, and the power of the Highest shall overshadow thee: therefore also that holy thing which shall be born of thee shall be called the Son of God."—Luke 1:34,35.

THE SCRIPTURES teach that the Lord Jesus was born with a human mother but born without a human father. Mary was a virgin when Christ was conceived and was still a virgin when He was born. She was with child of the Holy Ghost. The Holy Spirit came upon her, and she conceived the holy child Jesus. This is a blessed and vital teaching of the Bible.

Jesus was born of a woman so that He might be the

Son of man. Christmas ought to be a time of rejoicing, a time of praise, a time of devotion. But let us remember that all the true meaning of Christmas will be forever gone for anyone who throws away his faith in the virgin birth of our Saviour. If Christ were not virgin-born, then He is not God. If Christ were not virgin-born, then He could not be our Saviour. All Christianity stands or falls with the doctrine of the virgin birth.

If Jesus had a human father, then the Bible is not true: the book of Isaiah is false, the Gospel of Matthew is false, the Gospel of Luke is false, and the Gospel of John is false, for all these clearly teach that the Saviour, the Messiah, was born of a virgin, and was begotten of God, not begotten of a human father. There is no way to believe in the inspiration of the Bible if one denies the Bible claim that Jesus was born of a virgin without a human father. If Jesus were born of a human father and the Bible teaching that He was born of a virgin is untrue, then no sensible man living would believe in His pre-existence with the Father as taught in the first chapter of John. If He be not deity in human form, begotten of God, miraculously born, a supernatural being, no sensible person could believe that He is the Creator of the world, as claimed in Hebrews 1:2 and Colossians 1:16. If Jesus be not a supernatural being, God in human flesh, and therefore born of a virgin without a human father, then no sensible person could believe that He will be the final Judge of all the earth. If Jesus had a human father and mother just as other men, if He were not supernaturally, miraculously born, God appearing in human flesh, then His death on the cross could not atone for the sins of mankind.

All Christianity, I say, stands or falls with the Bible

doctrine of the virgin birth of Christ. The doctrine of the virgin birth and the doctrine of the deity of Christ are one and the same. The doctrine of the virgin birth and the doctrine of the blood atonement are so interrelated that they cannot be separated. They are Siamese-twin doctrines and neither doctrine can stand without the other. The virgin birth of Christ and His Saviourhood are one and the same doctrine.

Then anybody who denies the virgin birth of Christ is an infidel. He has already rejected Christianity. He has already denied the inspiration of the Bible. He has already denied the blood atonement of Christ. The man who denies the virgin birth of Christ may be counted a minister of the Gospel, but actually he is a brother of Bob Ingersoll and Tom Paine, a brother of every infidel and Christ-denier and Bible-hater in the world.

If anyone says that the deity of Christ is not essential, then he does not even know what essential Christianity is. To deny the virgin birth is to deny Christ Himself!

I. The Virgin Birth Is Plainly Stated in Scripture

That the mother of Jesus was a virgin when He was conceived, not having known any man carnally, and a virgin still when the Saviour was born, is as specifically and positively stated as any doctrine in the Bible. Please consider the following Scripture statements about the virgin birth.

1. **Isaiah prophesied the Saviour's virgin birth some 740 years before it happened!**

In Isaiah 7:14 the Scripture says, "Therefore the Lord himself shall give you a sign; Behold, a virgin shall conceive, and bear a son, and shall call his name Immanuel." The sign is given, as the preceding verse shows, to the whole house of David. A young woman was to conceive and bear a Son while she was yet a virgin and should call His name Immanuel, meaning "God with us". This Child, virgin-born, was to be God incarnate, God dwelling for a little while with men!

2. Matthew, the first Gospel, plainly teaches the virgin birth of Christ.

Read the following beautiful account of how God explained to Joseph how his sweetheart, Mary, was to become the mother of our Lord.

> "Now the birth of Jesus Christ was on this wise: When as his mother Mary was espoused to Joseph, before they came together, she was found with child of the Holy Ghost. Then Joseph her husband, being a just man, and not willing to make her a publick example, was minded to put her away privily. But while he thought on these things, behold, the angel of the Lord appeared unto him in a dream, saying, Joseph, thou son of David, fear not to take unto thee Mary thy wife: for that which is conceived in her is of the Holy Ghost. And she shall bring forth a son, and thou shalt call his name JESUS: for he shall save his people from their sins. Now all this was done, that it might be fulfilled which was spoken of the Lord by the prophet, saying, Behold, a virgin shall be with child, and shall bring forth a son, and they shall call his name Emmanuel, which being interpreted is, God with us. Then Joseph being raised from sleep did as the angel of the Lord had bidden him, and took unto him his wife: And knew her not till she had brought forth her firstborn son: and he called his name JESUS."—Matt. 1:18-25.

The Gospel of Matthew is recognized as the first Gospel written. The traditional date of the writing of Matthew's Gospel is A.D. 37, probably four years after the crucifixion. Even modernists all agree that the Gospel according to Matthew was the first one written. And this Gospel gives the longest and most detailed account of the virgin birth, and it quotes Isaiah 7:14 and announces that that Scripture was fulfilled! The simple explanation is that the child in the womb of Mary was conceived by the Holy Ghost. God was literally the Father of our Lord Jesus Christ and so Jesus was "God with us," Immanuel. The same Scripture plainly announces that "thou shalt call his name JESUS: for he shall save his people from their sins."

A Christ who is virgin-born is the Saviour. A Christ not born of a virgin, a Christ with only a human father and a natural conception and birth, could never be a saviour.

3. The Gospel of Luke, written by "the beloved physician", Luke, also plainly states the fact of the virgin birth.

Read the following in Luke 1:26–38.

"And in the sixth month the angel Gabriel was sent from God unto a city of Galilee, named Nazareth, To a virgin espoused to a man whose name was Joseph, of the house of David; and the virgin's name was Mary. And the angel came in unto her, and said, Hail, thou that art highly favoured, the Lord is with thee: blessed art thou among women. And when she saw him, she was troubled at his saying, and cast in her mind what manner of salutation this should be. And the angel said unto her, Fear not, Mary: for thou hast found favour with God. And, behold, thou shalt conceive in thy womb, and bring forth a son, and shalt call his name JESUS. He shall be great, and shall be called the Son of the Highest: and the Lord God shall give unto him the throne of his father David: And he shall reign over the house of Jacob for ever; and of his kingdom there shall be no end. Then said Mary unto the angel, How shall this be, seeing I know not a man? And the angel answered and said unto her, The

103

Holy Ghost shall come upon thee, and the power of the Highest shall overshadow thee: therefore also that holy thing which shall be born of thee shall be called the Son of God. And, behold, thy cousin Elisabeth, she hath also conceived a son in her old age: and this is the sixth month with her, who was called barren. For with God nothing shall be impossible. And Mary said, Behold the handmaid of the Lord; be it unto me according to thy word. And the angel departed from her."

Here again we are plainly told that Mary was a virgin (vs. 27), that she was engaged to Joseph. The problem of how she should bear a child without a human father troubled Mary, and the angel explained, "The Holy Ghost shall come upon thee, and the power of the Highest shall overshadow thee: therefore also that holy thing which shall be born of thee shall be called the Son of God." The virgin birth was essential were Christ to be actually the Son of God, that is, physically begotten of God and God in human form.

Obviously the doctrine of the virgin birth of Christ is as clearly stated as any doctrine in the Bible.

II. The Virgin Birth Is Also Taught Elsewhere in the Bible Besides the Explicit Statements.

We have seen that Isaiah, Matthew and Luke all expressly state that Christ was born of a virgin. But a number of other Scriptures, without using the term "virgin", clearly teach that Joseph was not the father of Jesus and that therefore He was conceived of the Holy Ghost, without a human father.

1. The prophet Jeremiah plainly foretold that Joseph could not be the father of Jesus.

Here is a most interesting study that will repay careful attention. Jeremiah 22:30 says of Coniah (also called

Jeconiah, Jechonias and Jehoiachin), "Thus saith the Lord, Write ye this man childless, a man that shall not prosper in his days: for no man of his seed shall prosper, sitting upon the throne of David, and ruling any more in Judah."

And only five verses below this statement that Coniah, or Jeconiah, should be counted childless, that none of his seed should prosper reigning upon the throne of David, the Lord tells us, "Behold, the days come, saith the Lord, that I will raise unto David a righteous Branch, and a King shall reign and prosper, and shall execute judgment and justice in the earth" (Jer. 23:5). And in the following verse we are told that His name should be called THE LORD OUR RIGHTEOUSNESS.

Although Coniah's seed should not reign and prosper on David's throne, the coming Messiah would come and reign on David's throne. So the coming Saviour could not be descended from Jeconias.

But what does this have to do with the virgin birth of Christ? Simply this, that this man Coniah was the ancestor of Joseph, the husband of Mary! Coniah, or Jechonias, was a direct descendant of King Solomon and King David, and reigned in Judah until he was carried away captive to Babylon. Now look at the genealogy of Joseph in Matthew 1:12, "And after they were brought to Babylon, Jechonias begat Salathiel...."Then Matthew 1:16, continuing the same genealogy, says, "And Jacob begat Joseph the husband of Mary, of whom was born Jesus, who is called Christ." Joseph was descended from Coniah (Jechonias), and if Joseph were the father of Jesus, then the Scripture plainly says that no one of this line should prosper, sitting upon the throne of David and ruling any more in Judah.

But in Luke 1:32,33 the Angel Gabriel told Mary about

the Saviour, that great Son she should bear, "He shall be great, and shall be called the Son of the Highest: and the Lord God shall give unto him the throne of his father David: And he shall reign over the house of Jacob for ever; and of his kingdom there shall be no end." Jesus, during His earthly ministry, of course, did not reign in Judah nor over Jerusalem. But Jesus is coming again, and the Lord God will give Him the throne of His father David, and He will rule over the house of Jacob as the Scripture clearly said. Revelation 5:10 says, "And hast made us unto our God kings and priests: and we shall reign on the earth." Revelation 20:6 says that those in the first resurrection "shall be priests of God and of Christ, and shall reign with him a thousand years." Christ is to reign on David's throne.

Was it clearly intended by the Holy Spirit who dictated the Scriptures that Jeremiah 22:30 should be used as proof that Jesus was not the Son of Joseph? Yes, it was obviously so. For after Jeremiah 22:30 says that no man of the seed of Coniah "shall prosper, sitting upon the throne of David, and ruling any more in Judah", the fifth and sixth verses thereafter, Jeremiah 23:5,6 say:

> "Behold, the days come, saith the Lord, that I will raise unto David a righteous Branch, and a King shall reign and prosper, and shall execute judgment and justice in the earth. In his days Judah shall be saved, and Israel shall dwell safely: and this is his name whereby he shall be called, THE LORD OUR RIGHTEOUSNESS."

No seed of Coniah should reign and prosper in Judah; but Christ, THE LORD OUR RIGHTEOUSNESS, shall reign and prosper on David's throne ruling over Judah and the whole earth! So Coniah, the ancestor of Joseph, could not be the ancestor of Jesus. Jesus was not born of Joseph!

106

2. The genealogy of Jesus, through Mary, does not give Coniah (Jechonias) at all, proving that Jesus was descended from David through another line, not Joseph's line.

We have mentioned the genealogy of "Joseph the husband of Mary", which is given in Matthew 1:1-16. But the genealogy of Mary is given in Luke 3:23-38. At first glance one might think that this was the genealogy of Joseph and wonder why the two were different. Matthew 1:16 says, And Jacob begat Joseph the husband of Mary. But in Luke 3:23 we are told, And Jesus himself began to be about thirty years of age, being (as was supposed) the son of Joseph, which was the son of Heli." Actually, the words the son, used the second time in this verse, are in italics, meaning they were not in the Greek at all. Actually there is no doubt that Joseph was son-in-law of Heli. The Gospel of Matthew speaks of Jesus as the King of the Jews, and so gives the genealogy of Joseph, His foster father, as an official record showing that, humanly speaking, He would be entitled to the throne of Israel. The Gospel of Matthew was more clearly directed to the Jews. But the Gospel according to Luke pictures Jesus as the Son of man, and gives His genealogy, not just to Abraham the father of Jews, as does the genealogy in Matthew, but traces it all the way back to Adam! So the genealogy in Luke naturally gives the actual human parentage of Jesus, that is, His mother Mary and her ancestry.

The Scofield Reference Bible has a note on Luke 3:23 as follows:

In Matthew, where unquestionably we have the genealogy of Joseph, we are told (1:16) that Joseph was the son of Jacob. In what sense, then, could he be called in Luke "the son of Heli"? He could not be by natural gen-

eration the son of both Jacob and Heli. But in Luke it is not said that Heli begat Joseph, so that the natural explanation is that Joseph was the son-in-law of Heli, who was, like himself, a descendant of David. That he should in that case be called son of Heli (son is not in the Greek, but rightly supplied by the translators) would be in accord with Jewish usage (cf. I Sam. 24:16). The conclusion is therefore inevitable that in Luke we have Mary's genealogy; and Joseph was son of Heli because espoused to Heli's daughter. The genealogy in Luke is Mary's, whose father, Heli, was descended from David.

Now note this interesting thing. The genealogy of Mary, and therefore the literal human genealogy of Christ, is not traced through Coniah (Jechonias) at all. It is not even traced through King Solomon, but is traced through Nathan, another son of David! (Luke 3:31). Jesus was actually, literally descended, through Mary, from King David. But He was not descended from Jechonias. God gave that additional proof in the Old Testament, before the Saviour was born, that Joseph could not be His father.

3. The Scripture repeatedly speaks of Jesus as the only One who was begotten of God, the only begotten Son of God.

This clearly refers to the fact that Jesus was born of a virgin, with God as His Father. The Scripture tells us that "Jacob begat Joseph the husband of Mary" (Matt. 1:16), but many Scriptures tell us that God begot Jesus Christ. Psalm 2:7 prophesies the coming of the Saviour and says, "The Lord hath said unto me, Thou art my Son; this day have I begotten thee." All Bible students agree that that refers to Jesus Christ. Now Jesus was in the very beginning with God. John 1:1–3 says, "In the beginning was the Word, and the Word was with God, and the Word was God. The same was in the beginning with God. All things were made by him; and without him was not any thing made that was made." If Jesus was in the beginning with the Father, then surely it could not be said that He ever had a beginning, in His pre-existent state with the Father. So when we speak of Jesus as "the only begotten Son" of God, we refer to His human beginning. On the mother's side we say that a child is conceived. On the father's side we say that the child is begotten. So when the Holy Spirit overshadowed Mary, God begot Jesus Christ, and therefore He is called the only begotten Son of God. No one else was ever physically begotten by God, as Jesus was, so He is "the only begotten Son".

The first chapter of John has much to say about Jesus as the pre-existent Word of God, as the Creator of all things. John 1:14 says, "And the Word was made flesh, and dwelt among us, (and we beheld his glory, the glory as of the only begotten of the Father,) full of grace and truth." When the Word was made flesh, that is, when Christ was made flesh, then He was begotten of the Father; and what the beloved John is here saying by divine inspiration is that they, the disciples, beheld the glory of Christ, and could tell by His glory that He was deity, that He was physically begotten of God! John means that anyone who saw the glorified Saviour on the Mount of Transfiguration, and again after His resurrection, as well as all the days of His ministry, would have to agree that Jesus had no human father, but was begotten of God and conceived and borne by a virgin mother.

It is true that once or twice the Bible speaks of Christians as begotten of God, but that is a figurative use of the term, and five times in the New Testament Jesus is called the only begotten Son of God. Those five times are John 1:14; John 1:18; John 3:16; John 3:18; and I John 4:9. So the Gospel of John and the first epistle of John unite with the books of Isaiah and Matthew and Luke in declaring the virgin birth of our Saviour!

4. Another reference to the virgin birth of Christ is given in Jeremiah 31:22.

There in a prophecy of the coming Saviour the prophet says, "How long wilt thou go about, O thou backsliding daughter? for the Lord hath created a new thing in the earth, A woman shall compass a man."

Certainly it would not be a new thing for a woman to conceive and bear a man-child. That is not what God means. No, he says, "The Lord hath created a new thing in the earth," an entirely new thing would happen. That is, a woman without any human intervention, without knowing any man carnally, would "compass a man", that is, conceive and carry and deliver a man-child! That virgin birth of Christ would be a unique event, a wholly new thing. Certainly this must be a reference to the virgin birth of the coming Saviour.

III. The Virgin Birth Is Implied All Through the Bible.

I have shown that the virgin birth is expressly stated in Isaiah, Matthew and Luke and that it is taught elsewhere very clearly. But that is not all. The birth of Jesus without a human father and His deity as a result is implied all through the Bible. I have mentioned three of the Gospels: Matthew and Luke expressly say that Jesus was born of a virgin, and John expressly says that Jesus was begotten of God and was the only person ever begotten of God, was God's only begotten Son. However, the Gospel of Mark leaves no room for doubt on this question. While it does not expressly state that Jesus was born of a virgin, it emphatically teaches that Jesus was the pre-existent Son of God which necessarily means that He was not the son of Joseph.

Mark 1:1 says, "The beginning of the gospel of Jesus Christ, the Son of God." The first word that Mark has to say about the Saviour is that He is the Son of God! And the first chapter only proceeds to the eleventh verse before it reports God saying from heaven, "Thou art my beloved Son, in whom I am well pleased." And all through the Gospel of Mark Jesus is spoken of as the miracle-working God in human form. That necessarily means that He was born of a virgin. Although Mark does not tell the story of the angel's coming to Mary and of the Saviour's miraculous conception and birth, that truth is implied throughout the Gospel.

So it is all through the Bible. In Isaiah 9:6 it is prophesied, "For unto us a child is born, unto us a son is given: and the government shall be upon his shoulder: and his name shall be called Wonderful, Counsellor, The mighty God, The everlasting Father, The Prince of Peace." Though this verse does not specially tell of the virgin birth of Christ, it calls him The mighty God, The everlasting Father. And that forever sets Him apart from every man-child ever born of natural generation, and necessarily compels a belief in the deity of Christ.

Isaiah 53 tells of the atonement; how Christ bore our griefs and carried our sorrows, how He was wounded for our transgressions and bruised for our iniquities, and how the chastisement of our peace was upon Him and how with His stripes we are healed. If one Man can stand before God for the whole race of men, and if one Man's suffering can pay the debt of all the sinners in the universe, then that one Man is no ordinary man. He could only be a God-Man, God in human form, begotten of God in a virgin's womb. That is why all those who deny the virgin birth of Christ likewise deny His deity and deny His atoning death, His substitutionary sacrifice for our sins.

Throughout the Bible we are taught that Christ is the Creator who made all things and upholds all things now. We are taught that He is to judge the world, and that the Father has committed all judgment to the Son (John 5:22; Acts 17:31). We are told that the same Jesus who was crucified arose from the dead. We are told that He ascended to Heaven and then two angels promised that the same Jesus should return again (Acts 1:9–11). Jesus Himself said, "If I go and prepare a place for you, I will come again, and receive you unto myself" (John 14:3). "In him dwelleth all the fulness of the Godhead bodily" (Col. 2:9).

The virgin birth is implied in every chapter in the Bible, and to deny the virgin birth of Christ is to deny that the Bible means what it says, to deny that it is the Word of God. To deny the virgin birth is to deny historic Christianity and turn one's back on the God of the Bible.

IV. Objections to the Virgin Birth Answered;

Unbelievers, haters of the Bible and rejectors of Christ object to the Bible doctrine of the virgin birth. But their objections are not sensible as investigation will prove.

1. They say, "It is only mentioned in two or three places in the Bible."

That is not true. We have shown that the virgin birth is plainly taught in Isaiah, Jeremiah, Matthew, Luke, John, and the first epistle of John, and is implied throughout the Scriptures everywhere. If it were only stated one time in the Bible, that would be enough for any Christian. But the virgin birth is as clearly taught as any Bible doctrine, and is often repeated.

2. Jesus Himself did not claim to be born of a virgin, says the modernist and infidel.

That is simply not true. Those who deny the virgin birth are not scholarly and they do not know what the Bible really teaches. Jesus clearly said, "For the bread of God is he which cometh down from heaven, and giveth life unto the world" (John 6:33); and then He said, "I am that bread of life" (John 6:48). Jesus said that He came down from Heaven. That could not be said of any other man in the world. That involved His pre-existence with God the Father and His deity, and necessarily presumes that God begot Him at His conception. Jesus plainly called Himself the "only begotten Son of God" (John 3:16). He was the only Man ever begotten physically by God. Jesus told Nicodemus that He, Jesus, was "He that came down from heaven, even the Son of man which is in heaven" (John 3:13). To the Pharisees, Jesus plainly said, "Ye are from beneath; I am from above: ye are of this world; I am not of this world. I said therefore unto you, that ye shall die in your sins: for if ye believe not that I am he, ye shall die in your sins" (John 8:23,24). Jesus said that He came from above, that He was not of this world as other men were, and that therefore He was God and that anyone who would not believe Him to be what He claimed to be, God in human form, should die in his sins! The virgin birth, the deity of Christ, and salvation by faith in Him, are all taught in these words of Jesus Christ. Certainly He claimed to be the virgin-born Son of God!

And all the enemies of Christ in His own lifetime knew that was what He claimed. John 5:18 says, "Therefore the Jews sought the more to kill him, because he not only had broken the sabbath, but said also that God was his

Father, making himself equal with God (John 5:18)."
Jesus certainly claimed deity, insisted that He was begot-
ten of God, that is, virgin-born, and came down from
Heaven, as no other man did.

**3. But scientists cannot believe in the virgin birth of
Christ because there are no scientific records of any
other case of one being born without a human father,
says some scoffer.**

Indeed! But we are not claiming that men are born
every few days without a human father! We are not
claiming that anybody else was ever born of a virgin. In
fact, we are claiming just the opposite, that Jesus is the
only person ever so conceived and born with a virgin
mother and without a human father. We are not talking
about an ordinary man, but a God-Man, God incarnate in
human flesh! If you should tell me that any scientist or
statesman, any genius or philanthropist of this day were
born of a virgin, I would not believe you. If you should
tell me that any of them rose from the dead, I would
laugh at you. The late President Roosevelt, for example,
was a man. He attained high honor, but nevertheless he
was only a man, born as were other men, and dying like
other men. There was nothing about Roosevelt to indicate
that he was God, that he created the world, that he will
one day be judge of all the universe. The virgin birth
would not fit Franklin D. Roosevelt nor any other man
who ever lived. It does fit Jesus Christ who is God in
human form.

A few years ago scientists announced that by the use of
an electric impulse, the ova of a female rabbit had been
stimulated into growth and development and that this
mother rabbit had borne a baby rabbit without intercourse
with a male rabbit. In other words, scientists were able to

induce the virgin birth of a rabbit. They have not been ble to produce the same effect on a human ova. But what scientists did by an electrical impulse in the womb of a rabbit, could not the Almighty God do in the conception of His Son Jesus Christ in the womb of a virgin? The virgin birth fits the nature and the life of Jesus Christ, and it is easy for anybody to believe who accepts Jesus as what He claimed to be, the Son of God who came into the world to save sinners.

4. But that would be a miracle, and I cannot believe in miracles, says an unbeliever.

A miracle? Certainly! But sensible scientists have long ago decided that only miracles could account for many things. Where did matter come from? It was created by a miracle, of course. How were the planetary systems arranged and balanced and set in motion? Unquestionably by some miracle of God. And how did life originate and begin? No scientist in the world now believes that life can come from dead matter of itself. Scientists believe that the earth was once a fiery mass where life could not exist. They know that now life is on this planet. Where did it come from? Without any other explanation possible, life came as a miracle of God's creation. One who cannot believe in miracles is an ignoramus and an unthinking enemy of fact.

A miracle, the conception of Christ and His virgin birth? Certainly! Christ Himself is the God of miracles. He worked many, many miracles Himself. He died for our sins, died as no one else ever died, and then miraculously rose from the dead. Miraculously He appeared to the disciples and then ascended visibly to Heaven. He is coming again. The Bible is a miracle. Creation was a miracle. Every time a soul is regenerated and made into a new creature, that is a miracle. Certainly the virgin birth of Christ is a miracle.

I heard Dr. L. R. Scarborough, the late president Of the Southwestern Baptist Theological Seminary at Fort Worth, tell in our class in evangelism in the seminary how one of his sons, only six or eight years old at the time, came home from Sunday School one day. "Dad, I don't believe that stuff they told us today about a whale swallowing Jonah," said the small boy.

"But, son, if God could make a whale and could make a man, why couldn't God make the whale swallow the man and keep the man alive three days in the whale?" asked Dr. Scarborough.

"Oh, well", said the boy, "if you are going to put God in it, I can believe it, too!"

So like that lad, if you put God in it, I can believe in the virgin birth. And everybody who puts God in it has to believe in the virgin birth. If Jesus was God come in human form, the only begotten Son of God, then of course that means He was born of a virgin, as the Bible says. Certainly that is a miracle, but the Bible is a miracle book, and Christianity is a miracle religion, and no one can be a Christian who does not believe in these essential miracles.

5. But intelligent people do not believe in the virgin birth, some ungodly teacher tells the innocent young people in his class.

He could not face an intelligent and informed Christian leader on such a question, but he sets out to break down the faith of boys and girls with immature minds, parroting infidelity because he is against God and the Bible and has not made any honest investigation. But what is true? Do intelligent and educated people believe in the virgin birth?

The answer is that every great creed in Christendom has stood for the virgin birth of Christ, from the Apostles' Creed on down to the Westminster Confession or the New Hampshire statement of faith. All the apostles believed, of course, in the virgin birth. All the great church fathers, all the reformers, including Martin Luther, John Calvin, and John Wesley, believed in the virgin birth. All the great teachers and preachers of Christianity—Spurgeon, Moody, Finney, Torrey—all the great Bible-believing theologians and evangelists and pastors and students have agreed on the virgin birth of Christ. The only people who deny the virgin birth are infidels who do not believe the Bible, do not believe in the deity of Christ, and do not trust Him as their own personal Saviour. Modernists, infidels, those who join Bob Ingersoll, Voltaire, Tom Paine, and Hitler, of course, deny the virgin birth. But no true Christian in the world denies the virgin birth. Great scientists like Sir Isaac Newton, Sir James Simpson, Lord Kelvin, Louis Pasteur, and statesmen like Gladstone, Lloyd George, Winston Churchill, George Washington, Abraham Lincoln, Woodrow Wilson, Herbert Hoover and William Jennings Bryan have believed in the deity of Jesus Christ and in His virgin birth. Everywhere that good men, profoundly intelligent men, love the Lord Jesus and believe the Word of God, they believe in the virgin birth of Christ as taught so plainly in the Scriptures.

Then let every Christian be happy in his faith. You have the best wisdom, the best character, the greatest fellowship of the ages on your side. And if all the world besides still denied the virgin birth of Christ, any Christian who has been born again, who knows Christ as a personal Saviour, would know that He is all He claimed to be, the virgin-born Son of God.

Let us teach the virgin birth to our children. It is a beautiful mystery, a holy mystery that they can believe and grasp. Let all of God's people give to the dear Lord Jesus the reverence and worship which belong to Him as the Creator of the world, God come in human form, born of a virgin, living a perfect, sinless life, dying for our sins on the cross, buried and rising again from the dead and ascending into the heavens, and one day to return again to receive us to Himself!

Wonderful Jesus

"For unto us a child is born, unto us a son is given: and the government shall be upon his shoulder: and his name shall be called Wonderful, Counsellor, The mighty God, The everlasting Father, The Prince of Peace. Of the increase of his government and peace there shall be no end, upon the throne of David, and upon his kingdom, to order it, and to establish it with judgment and with justice from henceforth even for ever. The zeal of the Lord of hosts will perform this."— Isa. 9:6,7.

YES WONDERFUL, wonderful Jesus! He is the marvel of all marvels. The dear Lord Jesus has in Himself all the glory of God, the power of God, the love of God, the righteousness of God! He is wonderful beyond all the wonders in nature, for He planned them all, created them all. The vastness of interstellar space, the power and wealth of all the suns, planets, and stars of the universe took only a moment of His time to create. When He stored the billions upon billions of atoms with imeasurable power, it was less to Him than the flicking of a finger, the flutter of an eyelid. Wonderful Jesus!

Jesus is wonderful in righteousness, because He is the very righteousness of God. He is wonderful in beauty, the fairest of ten thousand, because He painted every sunset,

119

every flower, created every jeweled dewdrop. He is the One who first conceived the grace of a fawn, or the majesty of mountains, or the awe-inspiring vastness and tumult of the seas.

Yes, Jesus is wonderful, but most wonderful as our Saviour. He made all life, and yet He chose to be born the Seed of the woman, chose to be carried in a woman's body, born in a woman's sorrow, nursed at a woman's breast! He Himself planted a mother's love instinctively in the heart of women, yet He had a human mother! He who is God of very God, one with the Father, became a man. He who made all the wealth of the world became poor, lived as a peasant, had not a home, was born in a borrowed stable and buried in a borrowed grave, and left no estate but a seamless robe. Yet this wonderful Saviour is on the right hand of the Father, assumes the management of the universe, hears every prayer, sees every need, loves every sinner, offers mercy to every heart! Wonderful Jesus!

The wonder of Jesus was so great that God could not keep it secret. So He promised to the first woman, when the first tears in all the history of the world were shed over the first sin, that the woman's Seed should bruise the serpent's head (Gen. 3:15). The news that God had provided a Saviour whom He would send into the world was too good to keep from poor, desolate, sinning men. So God promised Abraham THE SEED. "He saith not, And to seeds, as of many; but as of one, And to thy seed, which is Christ" (Gal. 3:16). All the sinning nations of the earth shall be blessed in that this wonderful Seed of Abraham should inherit the land of Palestine and reign therein (Gen. 12:3; 17:6–8). And this wonderful Jesus is as clearly pictured in the passover lamb in Egypt, described in Exodus 12, and in the snake on the pole to which penitent sinners might look and be healed, in Numbers 21:5 to 9, as in the New Testament, written after Jesus came.

So Isaiah, approximately 740 years before Christ was born, was inspired of God to speak of this wonderful, wonderful Saviour. In Isaiah 7:14 he tells us that Christ should be born of a virgin, that He should be called Immanuel, God with us. Here in Isaiah 9:6,7 we are told of this wonderful child born, this Son given, upon whom God will put the government of the world and of mankind, this Wonderful, Counselor, this mighty God, this everlasting Father, this Prince of Peace. In Isaiah 42:1–7 the prophet, by divine inspiration, sees Jesus as the mighty servant in whom God delights, with God's Holy Spirit upon Him. In Isaiah 50:6 Jesus is pictured. "I gave my back to the smiters, and my cheeks to them that plucked off the hair: I hid not my face from shame and spitting." Isaiah 52:14 tells of the marred face of the crucified Saviour, beaten and bloodied by the Jewish leaders, by the soldiers and the harrassing mob. Isaiah 53 tells us the wonderful story of how Christ purchased our redemption, bore our sorrows, and was wounded for our transgressions, and how God laid on Him the iniquity of us all.

Oh, the wonder of Jesus was so great that God could not keep it hid.

The predictive prophecy in the Old Testament in hundreds of verses foretold the coming of the Saviour, foretold that He would be born in Bethlehem (Mic. 5:2), His cry on the cross (Ps. 22:1), and a multitude of details of His birth, life, death, and resurrection. One who reads the Old Testament and does not see some of the many, many miraculous Scriptures that prophesy of Jesus to come must surely read with a calloused, unspiritual, and indifferent heart! It is not intelligent, it is not scholarly, it is not even ordinary honesty, for one to read the Old Testament and not find there prophecies which have been wonderfully fulfilled. It is only the bias of unconverted and perverted hearts that keeps people from seeing that this wonderful Jesus was foretold in the Old Testament.

And the miraculous prophecies of the Old Testament now wonderfully fulfilled in the New Testament prove that the Bible is what it claims to be—the very Word of God. They prove, also, that Jesus is what He claims to be, God in human form, the virgin-born, bodily-resurrected Saviour, the God-Man.

Let's make sure, as the Christmas season draws on, that we think much and delight much in the wonderful, wonderful Jesus.

I. The Baby in the Manger

It seems to me remarkable that in the Gospel much is made in Matthew and in Luke about the birth of the Saviour, yet only one incident further in the life of the lad Jesus is mentioned before He was thirty years old! We are told of the birth of John the Baptist, the announcement to Mary by the angel, the meeting of Elisabeth and Mary, and the praises that poured forth from Elisabeth's Spirit-anointed lips. We are told about the wonderful prophecies that Zacharias, the father of John the Baptist, made about Jesus. We are told about the troubled mind of Joseph, his comfort and instruction by the angel. We are told of the shepherds and of the angels who announced the birth of Jesus. We are told about the wise men with gifts from the East. We are told of how Jesus was born in a stable and laid in a manger, because there was no room for Him in the inn. We are told even of Caesar's decree which God used to bring Joseph and Mary to Bethlehem so that the Baby Jesus could be born, according to prophecy, in that City of David. How glad we should be that God made much of the birth of the Baby Jesus.

In Luther's Cradle Hymn, we have a little picture of the mystic beauty that surrounded the birth of Jesus:

Away in a manger, No crib for a bed,
The little Lord Jesus Laid down His sweet head;
The stars in the sky, looked down where He lay,
The little Lord Jesus, asleep on the hay.

Millions have sung the sweet message and hearts have rejoiced over the words of Silent Night.

Silent night! holy night!
All is calm, all is bright
Round yon virgin mother and child!
Holy infant so tender and mild,
Sleep in heavenly peace,
Sleep in heavenly peace.

Silent night! holy night!
Shepherds quake at the sight!
Glories stream from Heaven afar,
Heav'nly hosts sing Alleluia;
Christ the Saviour is born!
Christ the Saviour is born!

Silent night! holy night!
Son of God, love's pure light
Radiant beams from Thy holy face,
With the dawn of redeeming grace,
Jesus, Lord, at Thy birth,
Jesus, Lord, at Thy birth.

Now let us reverently consider what Isaiah says in our text about this Baby Jesus.

1. "...Unto Us a Child Is Born": the Human Jesus.

Here we have pictured the humanity of Jesus. I remind you that Christ had been present with God in eternity before the world began, but He had never been born as a child before. He had never become man before. So we are told, "...Unto us a child is born."

It is wonderful that Jesus had a human birth. Is it not strange that the infinite Creator should choose to come into this world, humble Himself, take on Himself the form of a servant, and become obedient unto death? Is it not wonderful that He should choose to come into this world through the same portals of human birth through which all of mankind enters the world? Is it not strange and wonderful that Jesus came into the world, not a full-grown man, but a child, a helpless baby? Oh, the dear Lord Jesus must be as human as any person who ever lived, as much acquainted with the trials and burdens and temptations of humanity. So Jesus was born a baby, and God would not have us forget it.

Jesus was rich, but now He becomes poor, that we through His poverty might be rich. Coarse, swaddling cloth wrapped the Baby Jesus as it would wrap babies in other peasant homes. The straw of the manger would prick the tender skin of the Baby Jesus.

Jesus, the Son of God through all eternity, has now become the "Son of man". And that is the title He used of Himself most often on earth. He became a man, was tempted in all points like as we are. Adam, the first head of the race, sinned and lost for all his descendants the inherent purity in which he was created. Now Jesus will buy the race back to God. "As in Adam all die, even so in Christ shall all be made alive" (I Cor. 15:22). Since Jesus was born as a baby and later died for the sins of the world, every baby born is exonerated from the guilt of Adam, in the records of God, and every little child, though tainted by inherited sin, is thus kept safe until he becomes a deliberate sinner, a conscious sinner. No one ever goes to Hell for Adam's sin. Jesus paid for all that. Now if a conscious, deliberate sinner will turn to Christ for mercy, His own sins, too, are blotted out. Jesus became a model man, the Son of man, the God-Man.

Jesus was the Son of Mary. He was also the Son of the Jewish race. Revelation, chapter 12, pictures Israel as a woman, and Christ, the man-child, as Israel's Son. But He is also the Son of the whole human race. The Gospel of Matthew pictures Jesus as Son of David and Son of Abraham (Matt. 1:1). But the Gospel of Luke pictures Him as the Son of Adam (Luke 3:38).

So, at Christmastime, every person in the human race can say gladly, "Unto us a child is born. "Jesus was born the Son of a human race, has entered into human sorrows, has met and defeated human weakness, and stands for us a new responsible Head of the human race.

2. Unto Us a Son Is Given: the Deity of Christ.

Jesus was born the Son of man at Bethlehem. But He was already the pre-existent Son of God. Before the Holy Ghost wrought the miraculous conception of Jesus in the womb of the Virgin Mary, and before Christ had ever become man, He was God, one with the Father. The humanity of Jesus dates from this human conception in birth; His deity dates from eternity. So when the prophet says, "Unto us a child is born," God speaks through him of the humanity of Jesus. When he says, "Unto us a son is given," he speaks of the God who left Heaven to become a man, God's Son who became the seed of the woman, the seed of Abraham, the seed of David.

Isaiah 9:6, "Unto us a son is given," is simply a previ-
ous statement of John 3:16, For God so loved the world,
that he gave his only begotten Son....

Make no mistake; Jesus was the Son of God long
before He became the Son of Mary. Christ was "the
Word" who was in the beginning with God (John 1:1,2).
He was in the Trinity, the Godhead, with the Father and
the Spirit, when God said, "Let US make man in our
image..." and then the Father and Spirit turned over the
job of creation to the Son. All things were made by him;
and without him was not any thing made that was made
(John 1:3).

> "For by him were all things created, that are in heav-
> en, and that are in earth, visible and invisible, whether
> they be thrones, or dominions, or principalities, or pow-
> ers: all things were created by him, and for him: And he
> is before all things, and by him all things consist."—Col.
> 1:16,17.

> "God...Hath in these last days spoken unto us by his
> Son, whom he hath appointed heir of all things, by whom
> also he made the worlds."—Heb. 1:1,2.

It is this Son of God who was the anointed of Psalm
2:2. The Hebrew word is Messiah. It is this Son of whom
God said, "I will declare the decree: the Lord hath said
unto me, Thou art my Son; this day have I begotten thee"
(Ps. 2:7).

Moses knew Him, for Jesus said, "...he wrote of
me"(John 5:46). Abraham knew Him, for Jesus said,
"Abraham rejoiced to see my day: and he saw it, and was
glad" (John 8:56)."

"Unto us a son is given." So John 3:16 says that "God
so loved the world, that he gave his only begotten Son..."

The New Revised Standard Version of the Bible makes a ridiculous and unscholarly mistake when it leaves out *only begotten* in John 3:16 and says, *only Son*. The unbelieving translators who have plainly said they do not believe in predictive prophecy in the Old Testament did not translate John 3:16 correctly in English because they did not understand what God said in the Greek. Their trouble was a spiritual inability to understand spiritual truth, which is inherent in all unsaved men. The Scripture says, "But the natural man receiveth not the things of the Spirit of God: for they are foolishness unto him: neither can he know them, because they are spiritually discerned" (I Cor. 2:14). What folly to have any unconverted man try to translate into English, truth which he is spiritually incapable of understanding in any language! God has many sons. We are told, "But as many as received him, to them gave he power to become the sons of God, even to them that believe on his name" (John 1:12). Again the Scripture says, "Beloved, now are we the sons of God..." (I John 3:2). So the same Apostle John, who wrote those two statements by divine inspiration, could not have written that God gave his only Son. But God gave his only begotten Son, that is, the only Son physically begotten of God. God has many sons, but only one unique Son who was physically begotten of God, miraculously conceived without a human father. That is Jesus!

In Psalm 2:7 God prophetically declares, "Thou art my Son; this day have I begotten thee." It is only the physical begetting of Jesus which can be dated.

Christ the Son is as ancient as the Father, and there can be no date set in the eternity of the past in which Jesus was spiritually begotten and began existence. But there was a definite date when the Holy Spirit came upon

Mary and overshadowed her and the human body of Jesus was begotten without a human father. Scholars may tell us that there are two Greek words, much alike, and that the word translated *begotten* in John 3:16 might have been the Greek word meaning begotten, or it might have been the word meaning only or unique. But those who understand the great truth of the incarnation know that the word could only have the one meaning, begotten.

Thus modern infidel translators brush aside the scholarship that translated the King James Version, and say that 'scholars have decided that the Greek word in John 3:16 simply means only.' But they are wrong. All the Bible-believing scholarship in the world knows that God gave His only begotten Son. It is silly and unscholarly, and shows a heart perversion to brush aside all the great scholars including Hodges, Warfield, Robert Dick Wilson, Machen, Allis, Scofield, Torrey, Broadus, Sampey, Robertson, Melvin Grove Kyle, Orr, Griffith Thomas, and a host of other saintly scholars, to play down Jesus, and to deny His pre-existence and His virgin birth! No, in Isaiah 9:6, as in John 3:16, we are simply told that God gave His only begotten Son.

How sweet it is that this Son is given to us. "UNTO US a child is born, UNTO US a son is given." Jesus is given to the Jewish nation. Jesus is given to the whole human race. Jesus is given to any poor sinner who will have Him. Better yet, Jesus is given to ME, and He is offered as MY SAVIOUR!

Oh, Christmas will have a sorry flavor for those who think of a Saviour but do not know Him as their own Saviour! Christmas will fall far short of the intended joys and blessings if we do not make this blessed Son of God and Son of man our own!

It is a wonderful Saviour who is given, and thank God, He is given freely to us.

Is it not strange that God did not bargain with man before giving His Son? Is it not strange that He would not set standards of labor or standards of holiness and character which must be reached by one's own power before receiving Jesus? How strange that it was not to some chosen few that He would give His Son! But that is not what God did, and that is not what the Scripture says. Thank God, Jesus is given. He is God's gift of grace. He is God's "unspeakable gift" (II Cor. 9:15). He is Grace personified. God had given the law by Moses, to show His holy standards of righteousness. But now grace and truth have come by Jesus Christ! Therefore all who will may receive Jesus freely and thus have God's own dear Son. Never a Christmas gift was given like Jesus Himself, and every hungry heart, every confessed sinner, every penitent soul may today look up into the face of God with contrite heart and receive Jesus Christ by faith. Jesus is already given; it is only for the sinner to receive Him to have everlasting life.

> *"He came unto his own, and his own received him not. But as many as received him, to them gave he power to become the sons of God, even to them that believe on his name."*—John 1:11, 12.

II. The Wonderful Saviour Shall Reign Over All.

Let us repeat our text again. Isaiah 9:6 says, "For unto us a child is born, unto us a son is given: and the government shall be upon his shoulder: and his name shall be called Wonderful, Counsellor, The mighty God, The everlasting Father, The Prince of Peace." Note that in the midst of this text the Scripture says, "and the government shall be upon his shoulder."

The following verse says, "Of the increase of his government and peace there shall be no end, upon the throne of David, and upon his kingdom, to order it, and to establish it with judgment and with justice from henceforth even for ever. The zeal of the Lord of hosts will perform this."

So, the Child who was born, the Son of God who was given as our Saviour, must take over the government of this world! "The government shall be upon his shoulder."

1. The Creation and Control of This Earth Are Put Into the Hands of the Son.

It is a remarkable thing that the creation of the whole universe was brought about by the hands of the Son. God turned over to Him the whole matter of creation, so that "...without him was not any thing made that was made" (John 1:3), so that "by whom also he made the worlds" (Heb. 1:2), so that "...all things were created by him, and for him: And he is before all things, and by him all things consist" (Col. 1:16,17).

Everything was made BY Jesus Christ.

Everything in this universe was created FOR Jesus Christ. All things hold together (consist) by Jesus Christ. He is the One who holds the earth in its orbit around the sun. He is the One who controls the magic of revolving protons and neutrons in every atom of material. He is the One who puts the spark of life in every unborn baby. He is as literally "the life" physically as He is the life spiritually. This world is made as the toy, the plaything, or the empire, or the realm of Jesus Christ. All the starry heavens, the planets, are part of the worlds which He made, which He controls, and which are for His praise and glory!

130

So, it was in the plan of the triune God that Christ should be the One of the Trinity who should come to earth and pay for man's sins. It was proper that God the Father should give all judgment to the Son (John 5:22). The Scripture tells us that God "hath appointed a day, in which he will judge the world in righteousness by that man whom he hath ordained; whereof he hath given assurance unto all men, in that he hath raised him from the dead" (Acts 17:31). All judgment is given to the Son. So, when Christians appear for judgment of their works, to receive rewards, and to reign in varying capacities with Christ, they come to "the judgment seat of Christ; that every one may receive the things done in his body, according to that he hath done, whether it be good or bad" (II Cor. 5:10).

All judgment is given to the Son. So when Christ returns to the earth after the tribulation to sit on David's throne for His millennial reign, all the remnants of the nations of the earth will be gathered before Him for judgment. "When the Son of man shall come in his glory, and all the holy angels with him, then shall he sit upon the throne of his glory: And before him shall be gathered all nations: and he shall separate them one from another, as a shepherd divideth his sheep from the goats" (Matt. 25:31,32).

Thus it is that when the unsaved dead shall be brought out of Hell and their bodies out of the graves and out of the seas, and they shall be called out before a Great White Throne in space to come before One before whose face heaven and earth flee away, they shall stand before Jesus Christ! God has given all judgment to the Son!

Oh, our Saviour has been so obedient to the Father, has so pleased the Father that the Father has determined to reward Him with all the glory and power that is the gift of the infinite Father to give. "Wherefore God also hath highly exalted him, and given him a name which is above every name: That at the name of Jesus every knee should bow, of things in heaven, and things in earth, and things under the earth; And that every tongue should confess that Jesus Christ is Lord, to the glory of God the Father" (Phil. 2:9-11).

Our wonderful Saviour—"the government shall be upon his shoulder."

2. This Wonderful Saviour Shall Reign on David's Throne.

Space does not permit us to go into great detail of all the wonderful things God has revealed about the reign of Christ on David's throne. But it is fair to remember that "he shall reign over the house of Jacob for ever" and that "the Lord God shall give unto him the throne of his father David" (Luke 1:32,33). It is fair to remember that Jesus is of the house and lineage of David and He inherits the eternal, unchangeable, unconditional promise made to David. God promised David concerning his son, "He shall build an house for my name, and I will establish the throne of his kingdom for ever. I will be his father, and he shall be my son. If he commit iniquity, I will chasten him with the rod of men, and with the stripes of the children of men: But my mercy shall not depart away from him, as I took it from Saul, whom I put away before thee" (II Sam. 7:13-15).

Solomon did not last forever, but his throne, in the future, will be established forever. David's house and kingdom shall be established forever. So says the unchangeable and perfect Word of God!

Jesus shall sit on the throne of David.

It is true that in some sense all of us now are translated into the kingdom of God's dear Son (Col. 1:13). It is true that one who is born again enters into the kingdom of God (John 3:3,5). However, in its fullest sense Jesus is now our Priest but is not yet entered into His kingdom. The Father has said to Him, "Sit thou at my right hand, until I make thine enemies thy footstool (Ps. 110:1). It is true that now the sign of Jesus is a cross and not a crown. It is true that now Jesus is despised and rejected of men. Many a heart and many a home will have no more room for Jesus this Christmas than they had in the inn the night He was born! But thanks be to God, He will one day reign on the throne of David.

One day Christ will be the Smiting Stone that will grind to powder the governments of this earth and He shall reign over the whole earth. One day the government shall literally be upon His shoulder, in a reign on earth. The heart cry of millions, "Thy will be done in earth, as it is in heaven," will be answered. Then the promise of the angel who announced His birth of on earth peace, good will toward men" will be perfectly fulfilled. Oh, what a glad time it will be when Jesus comes to reign on the earth!

3. Our Wonderful Saviour Now Has Absolute Authority Over Every Person.

Isaiah prophesied by divine revelation that "the government shall be upon his shoulder." Already God has made the hearts of all men subject to Jesus Christ. Those who rebel against God rebel against Christ. Those who obey God obey Jesus Christ. He has all God's authority.

When Jesus stood before the apostles and others on the Mount of Olives, before His ascension to Heaven, He gave them the Great Commission saying, "All power is

given unto me in heaven and in earth. Go ye therefore..."
No one is a Christian, surely, who has not bowed to the
lordship of Jesus Christ. Every heart who ever came to
Him, came to Him as Lord. If there be some rebellion, if
there be imperfect obedience, as there always is, then we
must acknowledge that that is not the proper attitude and
it is not the Spirit that God has put into the newly
redeemed heart. Jesus has all power, all authority. His
will must be our will.

We do not need to wait for a coming kingdom. We can
now make Jesus the King of our hearts.

Paul, moved by the Spirit of God, pleaded with the
Christians at Rome, "I beseech you therefore, brethren, by
the mercies of God, that ye present your bodies a living
sacrifice, holy, acceptable unto God, which is your reasonable service (Rom. 12:1). But that offering of the body,
that reasonable service is to be to Jesus, God's Son,
because all power is given to the Son. Our wonderful
Saviour must rule in the hearts of God's people.

To any lost sinner who reads this today I give solemn
warning that it is Jesus Christ, the crucified Saviour with
whom you must deal. There is no coming to God except
you come by Jesus Christ. He rightly said, "I am the way,
the truth, and the life: no man cometh unto the Father,
but by me" (John 14:6). No prayer will be heard from any
heart that does not bow to Jesus Christ and trust Jesus
Christ. No sin will be forgiven which is not covered by the
blood of Christ. No person has a right to call God Father
except as he may be born of God through personal faith
in Jesus Christ. The modernist who denies Jesus Christ
denies the Father. One who does not worship Jesus Christ
does not truly worship God. God offers no forgiveness, no
salvation, no revelation to any who deny and refuse His

Son. "The government shall be upon his shoulder." All salvation, all forgiveness, all peace, all rule, all judgment is put in the hands of the dear Lord Jesus!

We are plainly told, "Whosoever transgresseth, and abideth not in the doctrine of Christ, hath not God. He that abideth in the doctrine of Christ, he hath both the Father and the Son" (II John 9).

Oh, reader, today have you faced Jesus Christ and bowed the knee to Him? Have you acknowledged Him as Lord? Have you surrendered your stubborn will to Him? Have you made Him your King? Remember that God has appointed Him "King of kings" and "Lord of lords" and that "the government shall be upon his shoulder." Oh, I beg you, do not rebel, but "Kiss the Son, lest he be angry, and ye perish from the way, when his wrath is kindled but a little. Blessed are all they that put their trust in him" (Ps. 2:12).

III. The Wonderful Names and Character of Our Wonderful Saviour

Matthew, Mark, Luke, and John wrote the Gospels, the brief biographical sketches of the life and death of Jesus in the New Testament. But Isaiah wrote a Gospel of the Old Testament. With the divine Spirit of God upon him in mighty power, Isaiah was led to break into holy and exalted prophecy, "and his name shall be called Wonderful, Counselor, The mighty God, The everlasting Father, The Prince of Peace." What wonderful names and what a wonderful character our Saviour has!

1. His Name Shall Be Called Wonderful.

The word *wonderful* in English comes from the word *wonder*, meaning a marvel, a supernatural event, a sign, a miracle. So here Jesus is properly called the wonderful

One, the miraculous One, the One given from God, the supernatural Jesus.

I have no doubt that the Holy Spirit here meant to indicate the miraculous virgin birth, the miraculous turning of water to wine, the raising of the dead son of the widow of Nain and of the twelve-year-old damsel, the instantaneous cleansing of the lepers, the opening of blind eyes, the stilling of the storm on the Sea of Galilee, the miraculous power and knowledge of Jesus when He sent Peter to catch the fish with a coin in its mouth. Jesus is the wonder-working Saviour. One who would read the Gospels and try to explain away the miracles so plainly written therein is a fool. He is a wicked, calloused, perverse-hearted, unbelieving fool! And here I speak in the language which Jesus Himself used of such unbelief. He said to those who did not believe He had risen from the dead, "O fools, and slow of heart to believe all that the prophets have spoken." Those who do not believe in His bodily resurrection are fools, because such a Saviour must inevitably rise from the dead. Those who do not believe in His virgin birth are fools, because such a Saviour had come into this world untainted by the carnal and accursed inheritance of normal men and women. Oh, the Scripture rightly says that "his name shall be called Wonderful!"

Those who look upon Jesus as an ordinary man do not know Him as I know Him. Thank God, I have seen just as wonderful things done by the hand of the Saviour as those recorded in the Gospels. I know of black hearts made white, of drunkards made sober, of harlots made pure, of infidels made into saints! I know of those given up for dead who were instantly healed by His touch. I know of miraculous answers to prayer. I know of guidance and leading which turned out to be so infallibly correct that it was miraculous. Oh, Jesus is wonderful. I say it with deepest devotion and worship because He has proved Himself the wonder-working, supernatural, all-powerful God in His dealings with me and with other sinners. So His name shall be called Wonderful!

All the arguments about Jesus will be settled for any unbeliever who will, with a contrite heart, turn from his sins and take Him by simple faith as his own Saviour and his own dear Friend, Companion, Master, Lord, and Redeemer! One only need "taste and see that the Lord is good," to have his doubts flee away. One need only, like doubting Thomas, to spiritually put his fingers in the nail-prints and his hand in the side of Jesus, to find out that He is truly "My Lord and my God."

Oh, Jesus is wonderful! And that is one of His names. He is the miracle-working God.

No wonder that Jesus has ever done is any greater than the wonder, the miracle of regeneration. The sinner who comes to Him for mercy and forgiveness and regeneration receives a new heart. God's law is written in the heart. He receives a new nature, becomes a new creature. He becomes a partaker of the divine nature. He who was of the earth, earthy, now has a heavenly contact, a heavenly destiny. That which was born of the flesh has now been born again of the Spirit. He who was a child of this world, a child of disobedience, a child of darkness, a child of the Devil, has now become a child of God! Oh, the marvel of the new birth! Thank God that to us such a Son is given and that each one may receive Him by faith as His own wonder-working Saviour!

2. His Name Is Also Counsellor.

Some Bible students believe that the two words, Wonderful, Counsellor, ought to be together as one name for Jesus. Well, I believe that it is intended that the word wonderful is to fit all the other names of Jesus here recorded. He is the wonderful Counselor. He is the wonderful mighty God. He is the wonderful everlasting Father. He is the wonderful Prince of Peace. Everything about Jesus is wonderful! And so He is our Counsellor.

Jesus is my Saviour, but He is more than a Saviour. He is my Friend, my constant Companion.

Remember the Saviour said when He gave the Great Commission that we should go into all the world and make disciples, and teach these disciples to win souls and He said, "lo, I am with you alway, even unto the end of the world" (Matt. 28:20). So the Christian, in the will of God, is never, never alone.

Again in Hebrews 13:5,6 we are exhorted: "Let your conversation be without covetousness; and be content with such things as ye have: for he hath said, I will never leave thee, nor forsake thee. So that we may boldly say, The Lord is my helper, and I will not fear what man shall do unto me."

Again the Lord Jesus has said it; we are not alone. We will never be left alone. He said, "I will never leave thee, nor forsake thee" (Heb. 13:5).

> I've seen the lightning flashing,
> And heard the thunder roll,
> I've felt sin's breakers dashing,
> Trying to conquer my soul;
> I've heard the voice of my Saviour
> Bidding me still to fight on;
> He promised never to leave me,
> Never to leave me alone!

The world's fierce winds are blowing;
Temptation sharp and keen;
I have a peace in knowing
My Saviour stands between—
He stands to shield me from danger
When my friends are all gone;
He promised never to leave me,
Never to leave me Alone!

When in affliction's valley
I tread the road of care,
My Saviour helps me carry
The cross so heavy to bear:
Tho' all around me is darkness,
Earthly joys all flown;
My Saviour whispers His promise,
Never to leave me alone!

He died on Calvary's mountain,
For me they pierced His side,
For me He opened that fountain,
The crimson, cleansing tide;
For me He waiteth in glory,
Seated upon His throne;
He promised never to leave me,
Never to leave me alone!

You see, Jesus is the Counselor, the one always by our side, the one who never leaves us.

That is what Jesus meant when He promised the coming of the Holy Spirit. He said, "I will not leave you comfortless: I will come to you. Yet a little while, and the world seeth me no more; but ye see me..."(John 14:18,19). And then He went on to say, "If a man love me, he will keep my words: and my Father will love him, and we will come unto him, and make our abode with him" (John 14:23). The Holy Spirit is the Spirit of Christ, the Representative of Christ. Every Christian has the Holy Spirit constantly dwelling in his body. "If any man have not the Spirit of Christ, he is none of his" (Rom. 8:9). And all the comfort, the counsel, the guidance, the bringing to remembrance of the words of Jesus by the Holy Spirit are really the works of Jesus Christ, the blessed, wonderful Counselor who never leaves a Christian!

Have you, dear reader, claimed this part of the marvel, the wonder which Jesus has for His own? Do you lean upon Him daily for guidance? Do you listen for the still, small voice? Do you walk softly lest you grieve Him? Do you bend your will quickly to obey the wish of our blessed Counselor, the Saviour?

Oh, the Christian need never go without guidance, need never go without comfort, need never go in darkness. It is blessed to have one's sins forgiven and to be saved, but that is not all that Jesus can mean to God's children. They can have blessed, supernatural guidance day by day, comfort in every sorrow, companionship in every lonely hour by this wonderful Counselor, our Saviour.

3. Jesus Is the Mighty God.

I well know that arrogant know-it-alls may stumble here. How could Jesus be both Son of God and God? Well, both my father and I were named Rice, so I am a Rice and the son of a Rice. Jesus is God and the Son of God. Both are perfect deity. But I cannot perfectly explain the infinite God. I cannot put into human terminology all the truth of the Trinity. But what the Bible teaches I can easily believe. Jesus is the mighty God. He is the Creator. He is "the brightness of his glory, and the express image of his person," we are told in Hebrews 1:3. One who knows Jesus Christ knows God. One who has seen Jesus has seen the Father. One who has received the Lord Jesus and abides in His doctrine has both the Father and the Son.

The fact of the deity of Christ is taught so carefully in Hebrews 1:8, (quoting from Psalm 45:6) which says, "But unto the Son he saith, Thy throne, O God, is for ever and ever: a sceptre of righteousness is the sceptre of thy kingdom." God the Father calls Jesus, "O God." Jesus is God.

Paul, by divine inspiration, plainly says that we should look for Jesus, "the great God". In Titus 2:13 he says, "Looking for that blessed hope, and the glorious appearing of the great God and our Saviour Jesus Christ." Here both terms refer to the same wonderful Jesus.

Jesus proclaimed His deity very clearly to the unbelieving Pharisees. He said to them, "Ye are from beneath; I am from above: ye are of this world; I am not of this world. I said therefore unto you, that ye shall die in your sins: for if ye believe not that I am he, ye shall die in your sins" (John 8:23,24). Note particularly that the statement of Jesus, "for if ye believe not that I am he...." But the word he is not in the Greek, as is indicated by the italics in the King James Version. Jesus really said, "If ye believe not that I AM, ye shall die in your sins."

Back in Exodus 3:13, Moses asked God, "Behold, when I come unto the children of Israel, and shall say unto them, The God of your fathers hath sent me unto you; and they shall say to me, What is his name? what shall I say unto them?"

Then God replied, "I AM THAT I AM: and he said, Thus shalt thou say unto the children of Israel, I AM hath sent me unto you." I believe that Jesus, in John 8:24, is simply proclaiming that He is the I AM, the eternal God, the God of the Old Testament, one with the Father. He is saying that no one will ever be saved who does not accept Him as God come in the flesh.

Our wonderful Saviour is really "The mighty God".

I have heard some Bible teachers stress that one should not pray to Jesus, but should pray to the Father in Jesus' name, as if there were any jealousy between the Father and the Son! Actually, the Son is Deity as much as the Father. The two are perfectly agreed. The prayer that one hears, the other hears. The prayer that one answers, the other answers. Jesus said, "I and my Father are one" (John 10:30).

So if I feel like praying to the dear Lord Jesus, I do so. When He was on earth people regularly came to Him and pleaded for His help. He was the compassionate Saviour then, and He is the same compassionate Saviour now. God the Father was not jealous of His power then. Even more so now, He has determined that all power and glory and pre-eminence shall be given to His beloved Son. Oh, our wonderful Saviour is really "The mighty God".

4. Our Wonderful Saviour Is the Everlasting Father.

Here we have again stated the mystery of the oneness of Christ with the Father. We cannot ignore the fact that they are clearly two Persons. Jesus prayed to the Father. We are invited to pray to the Father. The Holy Spirit is the Third Person of the Trinity. Yet God would have us understand that Jesus partakes of all the glory, all the power, all the characteristics of the Father. So, here we are told that His name shall be called "The everlasting Father".

This teaching about Jesus is hinted at in Daniel 7:9 where in a vision Daniel beheld the thrones of the earth cast down and Jesus coming to reign. He said, "I beheld till the thrones were cast down, and the Ancient of days did sit, whose garment was white as snow, and the hair of his head like the pure wool: his throne was like the fiery flame, and his wheels as burning fire. Jesus is, "the Ancient of days." His hair is white as pure wool!

Again He is called the "Ancient of days" in Daniel 7:13, 14. Read that passage about Jesus.

> *"I saw in the night visions, and, behold, one like the Son of man came with the clouds of heaven, and came to the Ancient of days, and they brought him near before him. And there was given him dominion, and glory, and a kingdom, that all people, nations, and languages, should serve him: his dominion is an everlasting dominion, which shall not pass away, and his kingdom that which shall not be destroyed."*

See how well those words about Jesus fit with our text in Isaiah 9:7, "Of the increase of his government and peace there shall be no end, upon the throne of David, and upon his kingdom, to order it, and to establish it with judgment and with justice from henceforth even for ever. The zeal of the Lord of hosts will perform this." So Jesus is the Ancient of days.

The Apostle John, an old man exiled to the Isle of Patmos, saw Jesus. "His head and his hairs were white like wool, as white as snow; and his eyes were as a flame of fire" (Rev. 1:14). Surely the white hair pictures the eternal Saviour, ageless, and yet the Ancient of days. And He told John, "I am he that liveth, and was dead; and, behold, I am alive for evermore."

It was as "The everlasting Father" that Jesus spoke so tenderly to the woman who touched the hem of His garment and was healed in Luke 8. That woman had had an issue of blood twelve years, and had spent all her living on physicians. We suppose, then, that she was much

143

older than Jesus, who at the most was 31 or 32 years old in the flesh. Yet Jesus said to her, "Daughter, be of good comfort: thy faith hath made thee whole; go in peace" (Luke 8:48). Jesus called her daughter. To everyone of us He is "The everlasting Father" with a Father's pity, with a Father's strength, with a Father's provision. Everyone of us may look to Him boldly for all of our needs, for He is "The everlasting Father." Wonderful, wonderful Jesus!

5. Our Wonderful Saviour Is The Prince of Peace.

William Jennings Bryan had a tremendous oration on "The Prince of Peace."

First of all, in the meaning of the text, Jesus, as Prince of Peace, will bring peace to this war-torn, wicked, turbulent, restless world. It is only by the personal return of Jesus Christ to this earth that war will be forever banished. The dear Lord Jesus Himself will come riding upon a white horse, crowned with many crowns, to fight the battle of Armageddon, to destroy the reign of Antichrist, to set up His own kingdom upon the earth. We must remember that in the Lord's Prayer we are solemnly taught to pray, "Thy kingdom come. Thy will be done IN EARTH, as it is in heaven." Let us beware lest we prattle meaningless words and our hearts do not seek nor do not believe in the coming kingdom of Christ on earth.

We must remember that the angel promised to Mary about her holy Son Jesus, "the Lord God shall give unto him the throne of his father David: And he shall reign over the house of Jacob for ever" (Luke 1:32,33).

The work of Christ and of the church now is to make converts, to take out of this world system a people for His name. We are not to expect to convert the world. We are expected to win individuals. But Christ's reign will come

144

later. This was understood clearly by the apostles and given to us by divine inspiration in Acts 15:13–16:

> *"And after they had held their peace, James answered, saying, Men and brethren, hearken unto me: Simeon hath declared how God at the first did visit the Gentiles, to take out of them a people for his name. And to this agree the words of the prophets; as it is written, After this I will return, and will build again the tabernacle of David, which is fallen down; and I will build again the ruins thereof, and I will set it up."*

So, one day the throne of David will be occupied again, and

> **Jesus shall reign where'er the sun**
> **Does his successive journeys run.**

In that kingdom on earth there will be, at last, perfect peace. The wonderful world-wide peace under the reign of the Saviour is prophesied in Micah 4:1–5. Then "the law shall go forth of Zion, and the word of the Lord from Jerusalem" (Mic. 4:2). Then "they shall beat their swords into plowshares, and their spears into pruninghooks: nation shall not lift up a sword against nation, neither shall they learn war any more" (Mic. 4:3).

In that wonderful kingdom, Christ, "a rod out of the stem of Jesse, and a Branch...out of his roots, shall reign on the earth". We are told of the change of all nature:

> *"The wolf also shall dwell with the lamb, and the leopard shall lie down with the kid; and the calf and the young lion and the fatling together; and a little child shall lead them. And the cow and the bear shall feed; their young ones shall lie down together: and the lion shall eat straw like the ox. And the sucking child shall play on the hole of the asp, and the weaned child shall put his hand on the cockatrice' den. They shall not hurt*

nor destroy in all my holy mountain: for the earth shall be full of the knowledge of the Lord, as the waters cover the sea."—Isa. 11:6-9.

That is what Isaiah had in mind when he called Jesus "The Prince of Peace". The Lord Jesus Himself alone can bring peace to the earth. He will come with His sword, will put down every rebel, and set up His perfect kingdom and reign for a thousand, happy years of perfect peace on the earth. Then He will reign with the Father forever.

Jesus is not only the Prince of Peace in His role as Son of David, in which He will sit on David's throne. He is the Prince of Peace now, everywhere He enters in.

I have been an evangelist for many years. Among the tens of thousands of people whom I have seen come to Christ, there have been many remarkable instances where Christ became the Prince of Peace in a home. I have seen the drunkard converted. I have known when he called the estranged wife long distance and pleaded for her return. I have seen the family reunited. I have seen love blossom afresh and peace and joy unspeakable reign year after year in their restored home!

I have seen the distraught and tortured home, wracked by quarrels, suspicion, and rebellion, change to a little heaven on earth because Jesus Christ came in to dwell, and came in to reign. Oh, I would not forget to say that in my own heart and in my own home Jesus has been these long years the beloved and wonderful "Prince of Peace".

He is the Peace which every sinner needs. Jesus brings peace of conscience. He brings peace with God. He brings the peace of full forgiveness, of perfect fellowship, of happy security.

In Romans 5:1 is this blessed truth, "Therefore being

justified by faith, we have peace with God through our Lord Jesus Christ".

In Ephesians 2:14 we are told, "For he is our peace...." Jesus has brought us near to God". Jesus has made us accepted in the beloved. Jesus has paid our debt, and God has nothing against us! We have the blessed peace which one may have whose sin is covered, against whom God will not impute sin.

Sometimes I have heard people say to a sinner, "You should make your peace with God. It is true that every sinner should seek peace with God. But he cannot make peace. Thank God, Jesus Christ has already paid the debt of sin, and has made peace with God for us. We have only to accept and receive the sweet peace with God which is ours through the Prince of Peace.

Not only does a redeemed sinner have peace with God; he can have peace with his conscience. He can have his conscience purged from the sense of guilt, from the haunting dread of future punishment. He can have the peace that passeth all understanding. Through the blessed Saviour every Christian is invited to come and have all of his problems settled, all of his burdens lifted.

It is true that the mere fact of salvation does not settle all of our burdens. But, we are invited to bring every burden to God in prayer. We are invited, "Be careful for nothing: but in every thing by prayer and supplication with thanksgiving let your requests be made known unto God. And the peace of God, which passeth all understanding, shall keep your hearts and minds through Christ Jesus" (Phil. 4:6,7). So, a Christian can have the peace of God, keeping his soul as a garrison of soldiers keeps a city. Jesus is our Peace. He is the Prince of Peace. Wonderful, wonderful Saviour!

147

Oh, poor, troubled sinner, I beg you in Jesus' name that at this Christmas season you will open your heart to Jesus and let Him come in with peace and joy, with sweet rest and comfort, with eternal security and happiness that He alone can bring! One of the wonderful names of our wonderful Saviour is The Prince of Peace.

This moment this peace is mine. It floods my soul. It upholds me in the long, lonely hours of travel, days in hotel rooms, eating in restaurants, living among strangers. This peace holds me up in the midst of the attacks that come from modernists and other enemies of the Gospel. It upholds me and comforts me as it has for years, sometimes in poverty, sometimes in sickness, often in loneliness. It has upheld me in times of great blessing, and sometimes in times of failure and sorrow. Oh, blessed be God for this peace, brought by the Prince of Peace!

The Saviour promised us peace. He said, "Peace I leave with you, my peace I give unto you: not as the world giveth, give I unto you. Let not your heart be troubled, neither let it be afraid" (John 14:27). Oh, dear troubled soul, rest in Jesus today and have peace.

"I Accept This Wonderful Saviour as Mine."

Now that you have the sermon about a wonderful Jesus, I beg you to make the decision for yourself. Are you unconverted? Have you never known what it is to be born again? Has there never been a time when you came to definitely, once for all, trust Jesus as your own personal Saviour? If not, then I beg you in Jesus' name to accept Him, to trust Him, claim Him as yours this day.

God loved the world so much that He gave His Son. Jesus has paid sin's debt for us. He offers sweet peace. Will you receive Him? We are plainly told that, "as many as received him, to them gave he power to become the sons of God, even to them that believe on his name" (John 1:12). The moment you trust Jesus, depend upon Him, commit your soul to Him for pardon, forgiveness, and safety, He will come in and be your own wonderful Saviour. I beg you to receive Him, believe Him, and claim Him today!

If you will take Christ as your own Saviour, I beg you to sign the following statement, write it in a letter to me at once. Decide now; go on record now! I will write you a letter of counsel and encouragement.

Date: _____

Shelton L. Smith
Murfreesboro, TN

Dear Dr. Smith:

I have read Dr. Rice's sermon on *Wonderful Jesus.* I confess that I am a poor, lost sinner who does not have peace with God. I want Jesus to be my Saviour. This moment I turn to Him in my heart, I repent of my sins, I trust Him to come in. Here and now I give Him my heart forever and will depend upon Him as my own personal Saviour. I write this as an open confession of my faith in Christ. I will claim Him before others and set out to live for Him beginning today.

Please write to me and give counsel and encouragement in the Christian life.

Signed _____

Address _____

*For a complete list of available books,
write to:
Sword of the Lord Publishers
P. O. Box 1099
Murfreesboro, Tennessee 37133.*

*(800) 251-4100
(615) 893-6700
FAX (615) 848-6943
www.swordofthelord.com*